INTUITION

Dr Cate Howell is a general practitioner specialising in mental health and counselling for the past twenty years. She directs a multidisciplinary practice and regularly teaches students, professionals and the public. She has authored books on depression and anxiety, and co-hosts a radio show called *Health Talk*. Her website is: www.drcatehowell.com.au.

INTUITION

HOW TO DEVELOP IT AND USE IT IN EVERYDAY LIFE

DR CATE HOWELL OAM CSM CF

Empower

practical self-help tools by leading experts

First published 2013
This edition published 2020

Exisle Publishing Pty Ltd
PO Box 864, Chatswood, NSW 2057, Australia
226 High Street, Dunedin 9016, New Zealand
www.exislepublishing.com

A CiP record for this book is available from the National Library
of Australia.

ISBN 978-1-925820-31-7

Designed by Mark Thacker
Typeset in Miller Text Roman 9.5/14pt
Illustration on page 18 by Shutterstock
Printed in China

This book uses paper sourced under ISO 14001 guidelines from
well-managed forests and other controlled sources.

10 9 8 7 6 5 4 3 2 1

CONTENTS

Preface   1

Part 1: Intuition through different lenses   7

Chapter 1: A range of disciplines   11
Chapter 2: The role of intuition in decision-making   29

Part 2: Understanding and developing your intuition   43

Chapter 3: Intuition types   45
Chapter 4: The seven steps to intuition   59

Part 3: Phenomena related to intuition   149

Chapter 5: Synchronicity, premonitions and the third eye   151
Chapter 6: Healing   163
Final words   185

Acknowledgements   188
References   189
Index   204

PREFACE

The things we know best are the things we haven't been taught.
MARQUIS DE VAUVENARGUES.

This book came about by chance (or maybe it was more than that!). On a typical Melbourne day, I sat with my publisher in a beautifully grand Italian restaurant and discussed ideas for future books. As we spoke, I mentioned how I had attended a workshop the previous weekend with my sister on developing one's intuition. This ignited further conversation between the publisher and myself, and we both agreed what a fascinating subject intuition is. The conversation also raised many questions about intuition in my mind: how do we actually define it, how does it come about, how useful is it, what is the science around intuition and can we learn to be more intuitive? As you can gather, our conversation that day travelled in very interesting directions, and the result was this book!

I feel excited to be writing about intuition. My work involves helping people and I genuinely enjoy working with people and hearing their stories. In carrying out therapy, I choose to work in a multimodal way, drawing on a range of approaches, as one approach is not necessarily helpful for all individuals. Over the years I have learnt that I can be of service in many ways, through applying learnt knowledge, building therapeutic relationships, guiding individuals toward change, being compassionate, or tapping into my creativity and my heartfelt knowledge or intuition.

I have had a long-held interest in complementary therapies and the spiritual dimension of life, but these interests do not always sit comfortably in medicine. We are taught to utilise evidence-based treatments, and while this approach is absolutely vital, it raises a question in my mind: 'If we focus on these to the exclusion of all else, do we lose some of the art of medicine, do we forget the centrality of our relationship with our patient, or might we miss useful information or opportunities for healing and change?' The answer I believe is to take a holistic view, in essence to draw on the science *and* the art of healing.

My journey towards writing this book has been lifelong. As I listened as a child and absorbed ideas and knowledge from the people and the world around me, I became aware of the presence of intuition at an early age. I got to know my maternal grandmother well, especially as she lived with my family for a number of years. My mother would tell me that Nana seemed to know when people were going to drop in, or she would head to the phone just before it would ring. She would also know that a particular letter from a friend might arrive before it did. I was curious.

How could Nana 'know' what she did? And how did I know that a friend who had been overseas was back in Australia when she didn't let any of us know? At times the demands of study and work, family or personal life have taken my full attention and intuition has taken a back seat in my life, but it has always reappeared. I have learnt from experience that my intuition is most active when I am feeling centred and relaxed, or when I'm incorporating time for creative activities. Different experiences during my life have reminded me of the value of tapping into my intuition, and over the years I have focused on it and utilised it more and more in my professional and personal life.

In writing this book, I have applied a holistic approach to my exploration of intuition. I define intuition before looking at the available literature to draw out more on the existing knowledge and understanding of the subject. I also include experiences of colleagues and friends around intuition and incorporate my own experiences. Much has been written in scientific literature about intuitive thinking and how human interaction and perception are involved. I look at these aspects and also invite you to view intuition from a range of different perspectives. The essence of this book, however, is that it is a practical guide to give *you* the opportunity to explore your own ideas on intuition and take you through a range of skills designed to further enhance your intuition.

At its heart then, *Intuition* is an exploration of the *who, what, when, where, why* (the Ws) and the *how* of intuition. There are many questions to answer:
- Who has enhanced our understanding of intuition?
- What do different disciplines such as psychology or spirituality say about intuition?
- When and where has it been explored?
- Why does it occur?
- Why is it important?
- How do we develop it?

I will also adopt a particular metaphor for this book. I have always loved gardens and nature, and when I was young I had my own area in the garden for vegetables, flowers and various creatures. I adored the book *The Secret Garden*, and the film that followed much later, as the story incorporated both intrigue and hope. For those readers not familiar with the plot, two young children discover a secret walled garden in the grounds of an English manor, accessed through a wooden door. They find the key to the door and enter the garden. It is in a very neglected state so they set out to bring it back to life. This resonates with me today. I still love the feeling of my hands in soil or sitting in the garden with a cup of coffee. Gardens connect us with nature and help us to stay in the moment and enjoy it, inviting creativity. For these reasons, I have chosen the garden (and its key) as a metaphor for understanding and developing intuition. This book is all about finding the key to your intuition garden and nurturing it step by step so that it grows and flourishes.

I have divided the book into three parts:

1. In the first part, we consider a number of the Ws related to intuition, by looking at the fields of philosophy, psychology, neuroscience, religion and spirituality to see who speaks of intuition, what they have to say about it and why. I also draw on research related to the use of intuition in the fields of health, teaching, business and counselling.

2. The second part is devoted mostly to the *how* of intuition. It considers different types of intuition and is practical, focusing on how to develop your intuition and utilise it in your everyday or working life. You will be guided through *seven steps*, based

on themes from literature as well as a range of life experiences, my own and others. The steps include: making space for intuition, developing self-awareness and trust, meditation and mindfulness, tapping into creativity, accessing the unconscious mind, practising kindness and compassion.

3. The final part of the book considers phenomena related to intuition, including synchronicity and premonitions, and another very important application of intuition, namely its role in healing. It also provides some concluding thoughts.

Intuition is a very valuable part of life, and even though there is a great deal of thinking and science around intuition, there is still more to it than we currently understand. I have come to value intuition highly in all aspects of my life; in fact, it has become a friend. And I'm certainly not alone in feeling this way. I recently taught a workshop on intuition and one member of the audience came up to me at the end in tears, saying how wonderful it was to hear another doctor talk about using their intuition and how validating that was for them. They had felt it was a topic they could not talk about in professional circles. Another one said they were struck by the concept of there being evidence for intuition in decision-making and how science might be enriched by intuition.

My aim is to assist you to explore the concept of intuition more fully, and in particular to understand that it is accessible to *all* of us. I hope the book will enable you to explore how you might utilise intuition in your everyday life, and that it may be of use to you in determining your direction or choices in life, and in assisting you to help others.

Let's work together too, with the aim that it will help you to achieve some possibly unexpected outcomes. In fact, by the end of this book, I believe that you will be able to tap into a flourishing 'intuition garden' in your heart and mind!

Your 'intuition garden' journal

You might find it helpful to keep a journal next to you while you read this book. It's a useful way to jot down ideas that occur to you, and also a place in which to complete the exercises that will appear throughout the book. To get started, in your journal, write down your answers to the following questions:

- What are some of your thoughts at this point?
- What are your aims in reading this book?

PART 1

INTUITION THROUGH DIFFERENT LENSES

The best and most beautiful things in the world
cannot be seen or even touched.
They must be felt with the heart.
HELEN KELLER

One of the most challenging and yet rewarding areas of my work is couples therapy. In my work, I have been trained to view relationship issues with different 'lenses', so that I can, for example, be more open to the perspective of each individual. I have carried this lens idea with me throughout my life and work, and it has been incredibly helpful. In a similar way, in this chapter I will discuss some different lenses, or perspectives, on intuition. This will allow you to draw on existing knowledge and to consider what others have understood about intuition. We will draw upon academic literature as well as popular literature. The key points in each section are highlighted for ease of reference.

First, back to gardens and *The Secret Garden* in particular! You'll remember that when the children opened the door to the garden with their key, they found it in a very neglected state. To begin to restore it, first of all they had to uncover its existing structure and then do some dreaming and planning. Only then could the regeneration of the garden begin. Think about how *you* might regenerate or build a garden from scratch. You might dream about the sort of garden you want, as well as do some research on soil types or plants, and plan where garden beds or trees might go. This phase will involve deciding on an underlying structure for the garden and gathering the necessary materials. In essence, we have to follow the same process when we rediscover or develop our intuition. That is why this first section will provide some foundations in relation to intuition.

DEFINING INTUITION

It should be straightforward to define intuition; after all, it's something that most people have experienced. Some people refer to intuition as a gut feeling, their inner voice or sixth sense. The word 'intuition' is defined in *The Oxford Dictionary* as coming from the Latin word *intueri*, which means 'to look inside (or) to contemplate'. *The Collins Australian Dictionary* describes intuition as 'an instinctive knowledge or insight without conscious reasoning'. These descriptions suggest that intuition involves looking inside yourself and reflecting, that it is instinctive (unconscious) or protective by nature and different from reasoning with our conscious minds. In psychology literature, it is described as the apparent ability to acquire knowledge without the use of reason.[1] Hence, intuition refers to the capacity of knowing through direct insight, without rational analysis or deductive thinking.[2] This is sometimes referred to as 'knowing without knowing how we know'.

In writing this book, I interviewed a number of individuals about their views and experiences of intuition, and I share some of their definitions here. You might notice parallels in the descriptions provided by philosophers, teachers in the field of psychology and spirituality as you read on.

- 'Just knowing inside, before (something) happens, (with) no concrete evidence or proof.' — *Julie*
- A 'gut-feeling', and 'probably an evolutionary phenomenon, following on from instinct.' — *Jason*
- 'A sense of knowing, a different kind of knowing, versus knowledge, (more) subtle.' — *Rosie*
- 'A sixth sense, a feeling, in the heart or solar plexus area.' — *Lynn*
- 'A feeling, a knowing, a feeling of tuning in, being in the flow, tuning in to your Higher Self.' — *Melanie*
- 'A strong knowing, taking many forms; a gut-feeling, a thought, a dream, hearing a particular song; and [that it can be] spiritual.' — *Liz*
- 'We are born with instincts, but we lose touch with some of them ...'; 'Intuition is a state of knowing, incorporating perception and insight; and being intuitive is a state of awareness that stems from intuition'; 'We are all basically intuitive.' — *Sandy*

Chapter 1

A RANGE OF DISCIPLINES

I am still learning.
MICHELANGELO

Philosophers and scientists alike have endeavoured to understand and describe intuition for thousands of years, and many of the great spiritual teachers have referred to intuition. In this chapter we consider intuition from the viewpoint of philosophy, psychology and neuroscience. We also look at how religion, Eastern approaches and spirituality see intuition. You will come to appreciate some different 'lenses' in each of these realms, but also how there are some common threads or themes.

INTUITION AND PHILOSOPHY

Intuition has been a theme in philosophy since the times of the Greek philosopher Plato. Plato was a 'rationalist' philosopher; that is, he used reasoning. He believed knowledge included intuitive knowledge of 'the Good'. This 'moral' philosophy still guides our society and is based on the belief that our mind is able to intuitively make the distinction between what is right and wrong. Plato believed that knowledge of 'the Good' persisted forever in what he called 'the soul'.[1] The opposing 'irrationalism' also implies the presence of intuition. Many philosophers saw the relationship between intuition and reason as one of opposites; others saw intuition and reason as complementary in the quest for truth and meaning in life.[2]

Immanuel Kant (1724–1804), a Prussian philosopher, described intuition as a basic cognitive or thinking skill, similar to perception and related to time and space.[3] Later philosophers such as Arthur Schopenhauer and Henri Bergson favoured intuition, some seeing it as the key to cognition.[4] Rudolf Steiner (1861–1925) was a respected philosophical scholar who in the early twentieth century researched psychological and spiritual phenomena. He spoke of inner and outer knowing, referring to intuition as inner knowing and contrasting it with rational knowledge. Søren Kierkegaard identified three stages of human engagement in life, namely the aesthetic stage of living in the here and now and a life of pleasure; the ethical life with a sense of responsibility (right action); and a final or spiritual phase.[5]

ACCORDING TO PHILOSOPHY

- Knowledge includes intuition about what is right.
- Intuition and reasoning are seen as complementary.
- Intuition can be described as perception, related to time and space; and as the key to cognition or thinking.
- There is inner (intuitive) and outer (rational) knowing.
- The three stages of engagement in life are the aesthetic, the responsible and the spiritual.

INTUITION AND PSYCHOLOGY

Carl Jung (1875–1961) was a psychotherapist who focused on our inner world and psychological growth. He developed the idea that the unconscious and conscious parts of the mind were different, and he explored and wrote about psychic phenomena. Jung saw that people across cultures search for a myth or meaning to live by and came to call this level of the mind the 'collective unconscious'.[6] He classified human experience into four modalities, namely thinking, feeling, sensation and intuition, and described these as being like a 'compass' with which we orientate ourselves in our world. Jung described intuition as telling us about future possibilities, and he saw intuition as unconscious perception. He said that in different individuals, different modalities will dominate, such as thinking and sensation, or feeling and intuition.[7]

A contemporary of Jung's from Italy, Roberto Assagioli (1888–1974), developed an approach called psychosynthesis, which incorporates principles of Eastern philosophies. It is a transpersonal psychology or humanistic approach, a field concerned with the study of our highest potential and which recognises intuitive, spiritual and transcendent states of consciousness. Assagioli focused on how humans can move towards a sense of wholeness to enable them to respond to live more creatively and joyfully.[8] Psychosynthesis identifies the personal self ('I'), an unconscious, and a spiritual source ('Self' or soul). It states that we often get caught up with our emotions, thoughts and sensations, and this limits our ability to be guided by 'Self'.[9] Assagioli focused on awakening to the presence of 'Self'.[10]

Transpersonal psychology identifies a number of modalities by which information moves from 'Self' into consciousness, including imagination, inspiration, illumination, revelation and intuition. Assagioli defined a number of types of intuition:

1. sensory intuitions (visual or auditory) associated with conscious perceptions
2. intuitions of ideas
3. higher intuition (religious, mystical).[11]

He also reported that intuitions present themselves to the mind in several ways. He spoke of the opening of an 'inner eye' permitting the perception of some reality inaccessible to normal mental images, and of flashes of light associated with a feeling of authenticity. Assagioli said that imagination is closely related because intuitions often present as images, and he talked about inspiration such as that experienced by composers of music. Mozart reported that his compositions were for many years directed by intuitive inspiration.[12]

ACCORDING TO EARLY PSYCHOLOGY

- Jung described four modalities of experience — thinking, feeling, sensation and intuition — and said these are like a compass in life.
- He spoke of intuition as unconscious perception, telling us about future possibilities.
- Transpersonal psychology recognises intuitive and spiritual states of consciousness.
- It talks about a spiritual source or 'Self' which can guide us, and identifies three types of intuition (sensory, intuition of ideas, and higher intuition).

MODERN PSYCHOLOGY, THE BRAIN AND INTUITION

Modern psychology is based on research and is considered a science. In recent years, there has been recognition that thinking and other brain functions such as memory operate on both conscious (deliberate and controlled) and unconscious (automatic) levels. This is referred to as 'dual processing'.[13] Our brain is constantly active and processing information, and the unconscious houses much of our personal history. An elite athlete, for example, draws on years of previous training and experience (stored at an unconscious level) to perform well in competition. There are more and more books appearing on the brain and functions such as this, and rightly so, as it is truly incredible. Myers gives the example of something as seemingly simple as recognising someone's face, and invites us to consider what is involved.[14] We look at a photo of someone we haven't seen for years, the brain through its nerve pathways breaks the visual information down, reassembles it and compares it to previously stored images and recognition occurs. Amazing!

The brain has two hemispheres, left and right, and each has a range of roles. There is overlap in functions but, in general, if you are right-handed, the left or 'dominant' hemisphere houses the verbal and non-intuitive functions of the brain, whereas the right brain is the site of the visual, creative and intuitive functions. The right brain is very good at recognising faces, copying drawings and sensing emotions. It also interprets language and is responsible for empathic non-verbal responses, such as giving someone a hug when they are distressed.[15] It is important, however, not to see the two hemispheres as completely separate, as there will be individual variation and there is connecting tissue between the hemispheres enabling flow of information.[16]

Other brain dualities have been described, including two types of memory and learning. Some things are implicitly known (such as how to walk), whereas others involve explicit learning and remembering (such as learning to play a musical instrument). The right hemisphere is very active when dealing with a new task, whereas the left hemisphere is active in routine tasks.[17] Two ways of knowing have been described, namely experiential and rational. Experiential knowing is automatic, intuitive and non-verbal, and is different from rational and verbal knowing. Experiential knowing is more rapid and reflexive, and attuned to what feels good or right, whereas rational knowing is slower and is based on logic and evidence.[18]

Another duality is intelligence. There is academic and social–emotional intelligence. Let's consider the latter. One part of the brain involved in emotions is the *amygdala* (part of the limbic system). It operates before intellect comes into play, accounting for why we might have a protective 'knowing' (described as intuitive) on first meeting someone about whether they are trustworthy. This relates to the concept of instinct in our species functioning to protect us from harm. Another part of the brain, the *basal ganglia*, is also involved in social intuition.[19] Emotionally intelligent individuals are said to be self-aware and understanding of others' feelings and thoughts.[20] This is described as empathy, and it arises from the *brain cortex*.[21] Social psychologists view this skill as being related to reading non-verbal communication, such as facial expressions. Psychology views intuition as perception or information processing at its best (akin to the philosopher Kant),[22] and drawing on all the dualities described.

Sleep is an important function of the brain, and although we rest in sleep, there is evidence that our brain continues to problem-solve! In a study at Harvard by world expert on sleep Deirdre Barrett, students were asked to focus on a particular problem each night before going to bed. After one week, half the students had dreamt about the problem and a quarter had dreamt of a solution. Barrett says that in the sleep state, the brain thinks much more visually and intuitively. For example, Paul McCartney is reported to have come up with the melody for 'Yesterday' in a dream.[23] In the sleep state, the *prefrontal cortex*, which allows us to focus on a particular task, reduces in activity. This allows the thoughts to randomly mix up. There is less control from the left or dominant side of the brain when we sleep, allowing the creative right to be active.[24] Other research has demonstrated that REM sleep activates the emotion area of the brain, so that issues that are important to you on a gut level are prioritised. Hence, studies have shown that sleep can yield helpful and practical insights.[25]

Siegel, a psychiatrist who is interested in how relationships shape our lives and our brains, and who has an in-depth understanding of neurobiology and other disciplines, describes the structure of the brain as being like a fist with the thumb in the middle. The wrist represents the spinal cord and the top of the hand is the top of the head. The outer part is the cortex, responsible for movement functions and thinking.[26] One particular part of the cortex, the prefrontal area, has many functions including emotional balance, empathy, 'attuned' communication (that is, coordinating input from another's mind with ours) and intuition. Siegel reports intuition as seeming to also involve the input of nerve networks which surround our organs (such as heart and gut). He says, 'Our body's wisdom is … a neural mechanism by which we process deep ways of knowing.'[27]

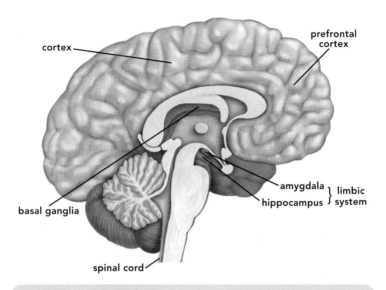

cortex

prefrontal cortex

amygdala ⎱ limbic
hippocampus ⎰ system

basal ganglia

spinal cord

ABOUT THE BRAIN AND MODERN PSYCHOLOGY

- Brain functions operate on conscious and unconscious levels.
- In general, the left-brain hemisphere is rational and verbal; the right is visual, creative and intuitive.
- We experience automatic experiential (intuitive) knowing and rational knowing.
- We have instinctive or social intuition (e.g. whether someone is trustworthy) and the capacity for empathy.
- Modern psychology views intuition as perception at its best.
- Intuition is housed in the prefrontal cortex of the brain; the limbic system and basal ganglia are also involved, as well as nerve networks around our heart and gut.
- In the sleep state, the brain thinks much more visually and intuitively.

MINDFULNESS

Over the past twenty years, a growing movement has occurred in Western psychology related to the practice of mindfulness.[28] Mindfulness stems from Buddhist and Hindu practices. The word 'mindfulness' is a translation of the Pali word *sati*. Pali was the language of Buddhist psychology 2500 years ago and mindfulness is a core teaching of this tradition. *Sati* suggests awareness, attention and remembering.[29] A current definition of mindfulness is paying purposeful attention to the present, non-judgmentally.[30] We spend a lot of time doing just the opposite in life, being mindless! How often have you eaten a meal and not actually been aware of what you have eaten? We may be at the beach around sunset, but our mind will be focusing on a bill to be paid or a relationship issue and we miss the sunset!

Mindfulness has come under much greater attention in the West in recent years. American psychologist Jon Kabat-Zinn has focused on developing and researching a number of treatment programs on mindfulness to assist with pain management and relieving stress.[31] Others have focused on incorporating mindfulness in the management of anxiety and depression and other mental health issues.

So how does mindfulness help? When we are mindful, our mind is in the now, rather than in the past or future. As a result there is less ruminating, less reactivity and a greater sense of peace and wellbeing. Let's explain this in terms of brain function.

Two different types of brain circuitry have been identified, namely 'narrative' and 'direct experience' (mindful) circuits. The narrative circuit involves parts of the medial prefrontal cortex and memory regions (*hippocampus*). This circuit is active when not much else is happening and you think about yourself; for example, when you sit outside at a coffee shop, sunshine warming you as you drink your tea or coffee, but instead of noticing your experience, find yourself thinking about a work-related problem or dinner that night. The narrative circuit is active for most of the day and involves planning, strategising, daydreaming and ruminating. There is nothing wrong with this circuit, but you don't want to be limited to only experiencing the world this way.[32, 33]

When the direct experience circuit is active, the *insula* (the region of the brain related to perceiving bodily sensations) and the *anterior cingulate cortex* (involved in switching your attention) become active. You are not thinking about the past or future, other people or yourself. What you are doing is experiencing information coming into your senses in real time; for example, sitting at the coffee shop, your attention is on the warmth of the sun on your skin, the look and taste of the coffee, and the sounds of people around you. You perceive more sensory information and you get closer to the 'reality' of any event. Noticing information in this way makes you more flexible in how you respond to the world, and you become less caught up in the past, your worries, expectations or assumptions, and better able to respond to events as they unfold.[34, 35]

A very significant piece of knowledge is that in the mindful state the brain demonstrates *neuroplasticity*. This is a term that refers to stimulating nerve cell growth, and when we practise mindfulness we are activating nerve cells in our brain and stimulating growth.[36] This is an incredibly important concept, as it means that the brain is always capable of change. We can change how we think, feel and behave. We can change our abilities. This makes sense intuitively — when we learn to tie up our shoelaces or to drive a car, we must focus our attention on the task at hand to the exclusion of all else. This is why several newer psychological approaches, such as ACT and Mindfulness-based Cognitive Behaviour Therapy (MBCT), incorporate mindfulness.[37]

Discussion about mindfulness also raises the concept of the mind versus the brain. I have described some aspects of brain function in this chapter, but how does psychology view 'the mind'? Siegel reminds us that the brain is an integrated part of the whole body and only one part of the nervous system.[38] He defines the mind as 'a process that regulates the flow of energy and information', both within the body and between people; and he goes on to explain that the mind and the brain correlate their functions, although we don't know the exact ways that brain activity and mind function mutually create each other.[39]

MINDFULNESS

- There is different circuitry in the brain for mindful versus narrative (planning) activities. Both are needed, as well as the flexibility to move between the two.
- When we are mindful, we are in the now and have a greater sense of wellbeing.
- The brain is only one part of the nervous system; it is the mind that regulates the flow of energy and information within the body and between people.
- We don't understand fully how the brain and mind function.

INTUITION AND RELIGION

Central to Christianity is faith in the Trinity; that is, the Father (God), the Son (Christ) and the Holy Spirit. Christians believe in an after-life (Heaven), and it is through prayer that they listen for guidance from God — one could say intuitively. St Teresa of Avila spoke beautifully of humans having an 'Inner Castle', or soul. She said that there are many ways of 'being' in a place and that many souls remain in the outer court of the castle with no idea what there is inside the castle. She believed that prayer and meditation enable us to enter the castle.[40]

There are many different forms of prayer across different cultures and religions, but interestingly, these different forms all involve going into a state of mindfulness.[41] Different religions place different emphasis on scriptures, tradition and spiritual experiences, and there can often be tension between these. Some religions teach that God can only be known in the heart or intuitively. For example, German theologian Friedrich Schleiermacher came to emphasise the role of feeling in religious experience. His views influenced many later theologians who believed in the importance of intuition.[42]

ACCORDING TO RELIGION

- Prayer is central to many faiths — a state of mindfulness in which guidance can be received from God.
- Different religions place different emphasis on spiritual experiences, with some emphasising the importance of knowing God intuitively.

INTUITION AND EASTERN APPROACHES

Eastern philosophies include Confucianism and Taosim from China, and Buddhism from India. Meditation is central to these philosophies and they all speak of intuition. Western psychotherapists have been interested in Eastern wisdom at different times, particularly in the early twentieth century and again in recent years, and we can learn a great deal from these approaches.

Taoism

Taoism is based on the notion that everything in the universe follows certain patterns known as the Tao or 'the Way'.[43] Confucius (591–479BC) was an educator who became the most influential figure in Chinese history. He saw the Tao as meaning 'the right way', and his ideas were based on the concept of *Ren*, or love of fellow man, with moral virtues cultivated through education.[44] In contrast, Lao Tzu, a contemporary of Confucius, believed virtue emerges naturally and that the way to overcome problems is by yielding or taking 'the Way' of least resistance.[45]

Buddhism

Siddhartha Gautama (563–483BC) was a spiritual teacher in India whose driving force was to overcome the suffering of mankind. He lived a life of meditation and austerity, and became the Buddha (the Enlightened One). He followed the 'middle path' between thinking that man's true self is eternal and taking the view that everything is impermanent and happens by chance. The Buddha attributed his philosophies to intelligence and reasoning. He saw humans as consisting of bodily form, feelings, perceptions, impulses and consciousness, with the person's state dependent on their moral action.[46]

The Buddha's notion of experience, however, encompassed a wider concept than ordinary perception. He observed his own past lives and the reincarnations of others during his meditations. Buddhist practices include mindfulness meditation on the body, thoughts and principles, with the goal of self-possession but non-attachment (to ego or 'I') and enlightenment. It is at this point that suffering disappears. The Buddha described the way to the cessation of pain as the Noble Eightfold Path, namely right views, right intention, right speech, right action, right livelihood, right effort, right mindfulness and concentration.[47]

Understanding the functioning of our mind is central to Buddhist philosophy and practice. The Buddha is quoted as saying, 'All things are preceded by the mind, led by the mind, created by the mind.' In Buddhism, 'mind' is defined as non-physical; that is, it is not body and has no form. The mind perceives, thinks, recognises, experiences and reacts to the world. It is described as having clarity and knowing or an awareness.[48]

THE SECRET OF THE GOLDEN FLOWER

Translated from the Chinese in 1929 by Richard Wilhelm and with a commentary by Jung, *The Secret of the Golden Flower* is a text based on Buddhism and Taoism. Wilhelm was fascinated by similarities between teachings in this text and Christian teachings, such as God being light.[49] A premise of *The Secret of the Golden Flower* is that humankind is part of the cosmos, and that the Tao or 'the Way' governs humankind just as it does heaven and earth. The inner nature of humankind is seen as coming from heaven, but it is separated into human nature and life. The word for human nature is made up of those for heart and mind, the heart being the seat of emotional consciousness awakened by the senses. This is referred to as intuition in the text. Man is seen as a spiritual being, with the soul rising after death. The 'Golden Flower' is seen as growing out of inner detachment from things and is eternal.[50]

ACCORDING TO EASTERN APPROACHES

- The Buddha followed the 'middle path'.
- Buddhist practices include mindfulness meditation.
- We must follow the Noble Eightfold Path (including mindfulness and effort).
- Human nature involves the heart and mind, the heart being the seat of intuition.

INTUITION AND SPIRITUALITY

The concept of intuition leads to questions about spirituality, or our relationship with Spirit. The word 'spirit' originates from the Latin *spiritus*, meaning 'breath', 'breath of a god' or 'inspiration'. There are different forms of spirituality, but a common thread is that the Divine is within each of us. A wise inner self or 'Higher Self' is referred to, and is seen to be a teacher or a guide. Christian mystics referred to the Higher Self as the Inner Light.[51] This is similar to the concept of 'Self' in psychosynthesis. It has been said that spiritualism presupposes that the mind has the capacity to relate to a realm without the limitations of time and space, and hence intuitive knowledge is possible.[52]

Many spiritual traditions, including Taoism and Buddhism, speak of the existence of an invisible 'third eye', which is believed to be the gateway to higher consciousness.[53] It is also referred to in the Christian Gospels (Matthew 6:22): 'The light of the body is in the eye: if therefore thine eye be single, thy whole body shall be full of light.'[54] The third eye is also referred to as the sixth sense, the sixth chakra (part of an interconnected energy system),[55] intuition or the teacher within. Some traditions have developed training methods to open the third eye, involving meditation and mindfulness. The third eye is also viewed as the mind and the senses working together, and as the portal to the inner realms.[56, 57]

Man as a spiritual being was highlighted in our discussion about Eastern philosophies.[58] A further example of this is Sri Aurobindo (1872–1950), a leading spiritual philosophy figure in India who was educated at the University of Cambridge. He differentiated the 'psychic being' (or individual soul) from the 'subliminal being' (several layers of consciousness between the soul and the mind and body). He said that 'paranormal' phenomena including intuition were accounted for by this subliminal dimension.[59]

Emmanuel Swedenborg (1688–1772), a Swedish philosopher and scientist, preceded Jung as a famous spiritualist thinker and author. Like Jung, Swedenborg was inspired by dreams and visions.[60] Boorstein went on to say that we don't have full understanding nor the instrumentation to measure possible dimensions outside our concept of space and time.[61] This is the realm of quantum physicists and metaphysics, a philosophy beginning with Aristotle and studying things 'above matter' and 'being' (for example, the possibility of eternity).[62, 63]

ACCORDING TO SPIRITUALITY

- Spirituality speaks of the divine being within each of us and of a 'Higher Self' or guide.
- The mind has the capacity to relate to a realm without the limitations of time and space; hence, intuitive knowledge is possible.
- Many traditions refer to the existence of the 'third eye' (akin to the 'inner eye'), a portal to inner realms and higher consciousness.
- We don't fully understand dimensions that exist outside our concept of time and space.

REFLECTIONS

We have done a lot of groundwork related to intuition in this chapter. Humans have a protective instinct. Intuitive and rational abilities (seen as complementary) have been recognised for thousands of years and are often referred to as inner and outer knowing.[64] Jung summarised human experience as thinking, feeling, sensation and intuition, and he described intuition as being unconscious perception related to future possibilities. His description of intuition as a compass with which we orientate ourselves in our world is particularly helpful. Transpersonal psychology expands the concept of intuition, expressing the idea that there is a Higher Self which guides us via intuition. It talks about three different levels of intuition, from sensory intuitions associated with conscious perceptions to intuitions of ideas and higher intuition (religious, mystical).

Common threads amongst the Eastern approaches include moral virtue, action and mindfulness. It is still relevant today to see human nature as being related to the heart and the mind, with the heart being the seat of emotional consciousness or intuition. Religion focuses on the value of prayer in accessing the soul and guidance. The concept of intuition also sits comfortably within spiritualism, and the concept of different layers of consciousness between the mind, body and soul has been suggested. We will come back to this idea of different levels of intuition in the second part of the book.

In understanding intuition, it is important to remember the functions of the two brain hemispheres (the dominant hemisphere being the rational mind, and the non-dominant the creative and intuitive half). This duality leads to two ways of knowing: intuitive and rational. Intuition appears to be housed in the prefrontal cortex of the brain, but it is also thought that it involves input from other parts of the brain and from nerves which surround our organs, consistent with the concept of 'gut-feelings' and 'heart-felt' knowledge.

I hope that this chapter has triggered some reflections in your mind and provided you with a foundation to the concept of intuition. In the second part of this book, we will return to some of the ideas drawn from these disciplines when we consider what may help you to develop your intuition further. We will revisit the idea that there are different types of intuition, the practices of meditation and mindfulness, the value of tapping into the creative part of the mind, as well as the idea of undertaking 'right action and effort'.

Your 'intuition garden' journal

In your journal, write down your answers to the following questions:

1. How did you find this chapter?
2. Did you see or identify some themes arising from the various disciplines?
3. Which ideas resonated with you?

Chapter 2

THE ROLE OF INTUITION IN DECISION-MAKING

Imagination is everything.
It is the preview of life's coming attractions.
ALBERT EINSTEIN

Can intuition assist us in our work and, in particular, our decision-making? Consider how you tend to make decisions. Do you rely on logical analysis of the situation or do you utilise your gut-feelings? My immediate response was that I use both, but I had to really take some time to think about when or where I tap into one rather than the other, and what is involved in making this choice. In the field of medicine there is a great deal of decision-making. We are taught to utilise knowledge and protocol to be able to diagnose a heart attack, for example, and to begin appropriate care. And while it is vital to draw on this knowledge, on many occasions intuition can also be highly valuable.

I was at a function early on in my career and there was an older man there who had been drinking. He stumbled and fell over. I wasn't nearby at the time, but one of the nursing staff came and found me and I went to assist him. He said that he had been well previously and insisted that the fall was due to having too much alcohol and that he wanted to go home. My gut-feeling was that there was more to this than was obvious, so I sought out his wife and asked how he had been over the past week. The wife reported that he had been fine in himself, but when I asked if anything out of the ordinary had happened, she said that he had fallen off a ladder a few days previously.

I knew in my mind and in my gut that this history was highly significant. I was concerned that he might have received a head injury from that earlier fall and insisted that an ambulance be called and that he go to the hospital. I rang through and spoke to a doctor there, suggesting that a CT scan of his head was needed. When this was carried out, a bleed around his brain from the ladder fall was found, requiring surgery. Had I let him go home, he may well have died. Was my decision-making based on logic alone? Certainly knowledge was a significant part of it, but I listened to my gut-feelings. Jason, one of my interviewees for this book, is also a doctor. He reported that he uses intuition on a daily basis in his work and has learnt to trust it over the years.

Larry Dossey, a researcher into paranormal phenomena, reports similar experiences by doctors and others,[1] and describes how his own curiosity was aroused when as a young doctor he had dreams that contained premonitions.[2] He interchanges the word premonition with precognition, gut-feeling or intuition.[3] He reports too, that soon after the tragedy in New York on September 11, 2001, stories began to emerge about people who had changed their travel plans at the last minute because of gut-feelings that something was not quite right.[4] This is a fascinating area and we will look at premonitions in more detail in a later chapter. Now we are going to look at what information is available in the literature about intuition and its role in decision-making. Most research has been carried out in the fields of nursing, teaching, business, counselling and psychotherapy, and so we will focus on these areas. However, no matter what field we work in, we can learn from this research.

NURSING

From the time of Florence Nightingale, nursing has been associated with compassion and caring. Nursing training has moved from hospitals to universities in recent decades and, along with other health disciplines, focuses on knowledge and evidence-based and technical practices. This no doubt has had many positive benefits for the profession, but we should also ask whether it has had any negative effects.

The nursing literature refers to rational and intuitive approaches in decision-making and raises the question as to whether the more technical approach encourages rational decision-making at the expense of intuitive processes.[5] Some of the literature refers to the concept of an 'Indeterminacy/ Technicality ratio', developed by French researchers Jamous and Peloille. This sounds complex, but is based on the work of sociologists who described professional work as being either high in indeterminacy (the use of subjective judgments) or high in technicality. It has been suggested that the rise of scientific or evidence-based practice has resulted in a greater role for technical decision-making rather than subjective (or intuitive) decision-making in healthcare.[6]

So what approach do the nurses themselves prefer? Several studies have considered this question, including one by Michael Traynor and colleagues who carried out discussion groups with experienced nurses. The nurses indicated that their decision-making was influenced by both subjective and technical features. However, they relied more on their personal 'experience' in the final stages of decision-making. These results challenged the view that clinical decision-making should rely solely on technical approaches. Findings of this study supported the idea of taking a holistic approach; that is, drawing on intuition and subjective knowledge, as well as evidence-based approaches, to meet the needs of patients.[7]

In a further study, European nurses were surveyed about their use of technical versus intuitive styles in relation to decision-making.[8] They found that the nurses used both styles. Interestingly, the researchers also looked at the links between the nurses' preferred style and their personal attributes. They found that conscientiousness was a strong predictor of a preference for technical thinking, whereas agreeableness and openness to experience were predictors of a preference for intuitive thinking. They also noted that the nurses relied on personal 'experience' in their final decision-making, just as the previous study had found.[9]

In another study, UK researcher Ian Welsh explored the experience of intuition in emergency nursing, with the findings suggesting that the use of intuition in clinical practice should be recognised as valid.[10] Anita Smith, a maternal nursing academic, also discusses intuition as a legitimate form of knowledge, rather than solely as a trait that arises from expertise.[11]

NURSING

- Professional work can be high in subjectivity or in technicality (that is, intuition versus rational approaches).
- Evidence-based practice has led to a greater role for rational decision-making.
- However, in caring for patients, a holistic approach to decision-making is possible, drawing on intuition as well as rational approaches.
- Nurses use both rational and intuitive styles of thinking, but they rely more on their personal 'experience' in the final stages of decision-making.
- The use of intuition in clinical practice should be recognised as valid.

TEACHING

The concept of intuition is known and used throughout the world in teaching. The experiences of teachers in relation to 'intuition-in-action' has been explored, and experienced teachers have spoken of the importance of intuition in their teaching.[12] One teacher said about dealing with particular classroom situations: 'Afterwards, you wonder where on earth you got that from.'[13] The teacher's frame of mind has been identified as a key theme in research, and the ability to utilise intuition has been found to relate to their own wellbeing (how happy, stressed, tired they are). Teachers believed they were more intuitive when they were 'being there'; that is, not thinking of something else or being occupied with other things, as this enabled them to be sensitive and aware of others' experiences. This was encapsulated by one teacher who said, 'You can't assume [intuition] is going to function by itself, you must be present every single moment.'[14] This 'being there' frame of mind is, of course, consistent with mindfulness.

Research needs to be translated into the classroom setting, so studies have been done on the importance of intuitive processes when teachers are working with groups. For example, Thomas described what teachers do 'in the heat of the moment' as being very much intuitive.[15] They may respond to a situation, only later taking a moment to reflect on what was going on and why they did what they did.[16] Thomas also stresses the importance of being focused on the person in facilitation, enabling intuitive process to occur and testing out ideas that arise in the group. Creating a 'playful, cooperative and non-judgmental (environment), as well as being purposeful', is recommended.[17]

The role of intuition in decision-making has also been studied in the field of teacher education. Malcolm Gladwell, author of *Blink*, refers to the part of our brain that allows for fast decision-making as the 'adaptive unconscious', reporting that it works quickly to process the large amount of information that comes into our brain.[18] He describes how making decisions quickly can in some cases be as effective as making decisions deliberately, and that our quick judgments and 'first impressions can be educated and controlled'.[19] Gladwell explains that rapid decision-making uses a process called 'thin slicing', or 'the ability of our unconscious to find patterns in situations and behaviour based on very narrow slices of experience'.[20]

Researcher Guy Claxton, a leader in this field, describes intuition as an unconscious knowing, involving a holistic view of a teaching situation, and with a feeling of rightness. He also suggests that intuition can be extremely useful but that the information it provides should be treated as a theory rather than 'the truth'.[21] He warns, however, that viewing intuition as a guide rather than the truth might be difficult because of the subjective feeling of 'rightness' associated with intuition.[22] In summary, the researchers agree that intuition can provide valuable information and insights to be tested, and people can be taught how to make it more reliable.

TEACHING

- Intuition is used all over the world in teaching.
- The ability to utilise it relates to the teacher's own wellbeing.
- Being mindful is important.
- Intuition provides a valuable source of theories that can be tested.
- Making decisions very quickly can be as effective as making decisions deliberately.
- Intuition can be of value, and people can be taught how to make it more reliable.

BUSINESS

In the business field, there are a number of writers who consider the decision-making process and the role of intuition. Organisational researchers Erik Dane and Michael Pratt propose four characteristics of intuition:[23]

1. It is a non-conscious process.
2. It involves holistic associations or the matching of environmental stimuli with deeply held categories, patterns or features.

3. These are produced rapidly.

4. Intuition results in emotionally charged judgments.

These authors suggest a variety of reasons for why we are likely to use our intuition rather than solely relying on reasoning, including positive moods, individual differences in thinking style (more intuitive styles), and picking up on bodily cues.[24] The literature suggests that managers use intuition in a range of different ways; for example, moving backwards and forwards between rational analysis and intuition.[25] Other researchers explore ways that educators can teach intuition to business students, such as journalling intuitive experiences, mapping decision-making, scrutinising and giving feedback on intuitive decisions, being aware of potential biases and using mental relaxation.[26]

Management expert Weston Agor focuses on the importance of using intuition in top-level management, outlining that senior managers use intuition when a high level of uncertainty exists and little previous precedent, when 'facts' are limited or do not clearly point the way to go, when data are of little use, when several possible and appropriate solutions exist to choose from, when time is limited and there is pressure to come up with the right decision.[27]

BUSINESS

- Intuition is a rapid, non-conscious process.
- We use our intuition when we are in a positive mood, when we have a more intuitive thinking style or readily pick up bodily cues.
- We may move backwards and forwards between

intuitive and rational thinking.

- Educators can teach intuition through journalling, mapping decision-making and using mental relaxation.
- Managers use intuition when a high level of uncertainty exists or when there is pressure to come up with the right decision.

COUNSELLING AND PSYCHOTHERAPY

This is a very broad area that includes a range of therapeutic approaches. At their essence is engagement and conversation between two persons.[28] The role of intuition in decision-making in the psychiatry field has been reviewed by a number of researchers. Given the growing body of information about intuition in the cognitive psychology and counselling literature, counselling teachers Sheri Eisengart and Christopher Faiver suggest that there are reasonable grounds for incorporating intuition in practice, to guide and modify psychiatric diagnosis.[29] They comment that intuition is a non-conscious cognitive process operating in a rapid manner and often out-performing more conscious thinking.[30] Heikki Piha, a Finnish psychoanalyist, views intuition as important to creativity and everyday life and 'an essential element of the psychoanalyst', serving like a 'radar' to create contacts with the inner world of the client.[31]

Another analyst, Lynne Laub, views intuition as a useful tool in therapy. She describes 'listening intuitively' as not only actively listening but also recognising symbols, metaphors, dreams, non-verbal communications and sensory perceptions, which can be keys to the client's unconscious emotional material.[32] She explains that it takes all of our sensory perceptions to listen to what is unknown, and that intuitive listening assists us to be alerted to something more happening than simply what is being spoken about.[33]

Analyst Theodora La Quercia suggests that we can train ourselves to be attuned to our unconscious communications. Analysts sit quietly and listen to their client, and as they do so they notice their own thoughts and feelings. La Quercia suggests that this process involves more than logical analysis,[34] and that the practitioner's highest cortical centre in the brain (which holds theoretical knowledge) works with the deeper limbic structures 'so that our intuitive knowledge may become fully integrated with our theoretical knowledge, and thus help us to resonate better with our patients'.[35]

In the field of psychotherapy, Bayard Doge Rea views reasoning as having an essential place in clinical psychology, but believes that it currently 'seems to override other potentially valuable elements of a balanced therapeutic approach' such as intuition.[36] He reports that intuition is an underestimated tool and is not well recognised among clinicians,[37] before going on to say that intuition 'seems to flourish within an open and creative therapeutic context, and where a therapist is receptive to all messages from the client'.[38] He advocates a balance between reason and intuition to improve client care.

The counselling literature considers intuition to be central to the process. British psychotherapist Sherly Williams refers to intuition in counsellors as usually being expressed in terms of learning through experience and involving the development of wisdom over time. This enables the counsellor to act at times without necessarily knowing why. It also involves being fully present with the client. Williams' paper interestingly refers to the 'wholeness of action', saying that rather than breaking the process down into cognition and so on, experiences are brought together to produce knowing.[39] Along the same lines, an article by researcher Alex Broom in the field of cancer care refers to an interesting model called 'bricolage', or piecing together, in which various practices are combined to provide the best therapeutic approach.[40] Subjective experiences are included in the therapist's 'toolbox', as well as scientific knowledge.[41]

Empathy, or entering into and understanding a person's private world as they perceive it,[42] is central to all counselling or therapy. Individuals trained in this area will remember being taught about empathy, learning how to develop it and how to communicate it to their clients. Piha views empathy as leading to intuition. Therapists will sometimes refer to 'aha' reactions within themselves when the key issue or emotion related to the client has been identified. Piha very much links this to intuition.[43]

COUNSELLING AND PSYCHOTHERAPY

- Intuition serves like a 'radar' to connect with the inner world of the client.
- Listening intuitively may involve recognising symbols, dreams and related phenomena.
- Therapists can also train themselves to be attuned to their own unconscious communications.
- Intuition flourishes when there is an open and creative setting, when a therapist is receptive and is fully present with their client.
- Empathy or understanding a person's world as they perceive it leads to intuition.

REFLECTIONS

Some of the key points in this chapter relate to drawing on both rational and intuitive knowledge to meet the needs of clients. This is preferred in the area of nursing and teaching. It has been suggested that teachers and those in business treat information from intuition as hypotheses to be tested. Various models of how we use intuition in decision-making have been suggested, such as moving backwards and forwards between rational thinking and intuition. Teachers utilise intuition more when they have a sense of wellbeing and when they're fully present or mindful. This has implications as to how we can enhance our intuition. Ways that educators can teach intuition, such as journalling or mental relaxation, have also been outlined and we will draw on these ideas later in the book.

As a therapist, I find the literature on intuition in therapy fascinating. Reflecting Jung's idea of intuition being like a 'compass', the description of intuition serving like a 'radar' to create contacts with the inner world of the client is particularly useful. 'Intuitive listening' was described together with its role in helping to identify what is not being spoken about. The literature encourages integration of intuitive and theoretical knowledge to better resonate with our clients. Several authors spoke of taking a holistic approach. The proposed model of 'bricolage', or piecing together various ideologies to provide the optimum therapeutic approach, sits comfortably with a holistic or multimodal therapeutic model. Further ideas on healing will be explored in the last section of the book.

Your 'intuition garden' journal

Take some time to reflect on whether any of the suggestions of researchers resonate in your field of work or with other areas in life. Write your thoughts in your journal.

PART 2

UNDERSTANDING AND DEVELOPING YOUR INTUITION

Where there is great love, there are always miracles.
WILLA CATHER

Welcome to Part 2! This section is devoted to understanding more about the *how* of intuition and to developing intuition skills. In earlier discussion, we talked about different levels, or layers, of intuition — from instinct and sensory intuition to intuition of ideas and 'higher intuition'. This concept of layers provides a useful framework for understanding intuition as intuitive experiences can have many different qualities, ranging from a protective 'gut-feeling' to sensory experiences, intuitive thought, a flash of knowing or an inspirational experience. Another way of viewing the development of intuition is through the concept of *relationship*. Humans crave connectedness, whether with self or others or through a sense of spiritual connectedness. Intuition involves relationship with self and with our inner knowing, and for some it can involve a sense of transcendental knowing. It also involves relationships with others through being mindful and empathic.

This section is therefore all about:

- assisting you to understand and develop the different levels of your intuition
- developing your relationship with self and your inner knowing, and with others.

I will guide you through an exploration of the different types of sensory intuition in Chapter 3, and you will have the chance to do some exercises to help identify which type of sensory intuition you relate to the most. This knowledge and experience will assist you to understand how you might notice and enhance your intuition.

In Chapter 4, you will be guided through a series of *seven steps* designed to assist you in developing your intuition. These steps have arisen from themes that stood out in the literature presented in Part 1, and from life learning and experience. They are key in enhancing your intuition. Returning to the garden metaphor, if Part 1 represented the foundations of your garden, then Part 2 relates to establishing your garden. Gardeners will know that this is an exciting phase as you start to get your hands dirty and do more work. At the outset there might be areas to clear of bushes or weeds, or you might need to enrich the soil or bring in extra soil. This is a creative time too, planning what trees or plants you will incorporate and how. Will there be a garden bench or fountain, or even a quiet corner for meditation? There is the satisfaction of putting in the plants, building the features and seeing your ideas come to fruition. So enjoy this section as you grow your intuition.

Chapter 3

INTUITION TYPES

At the centre of your being you have the answer;
you know who you are and you know what you want.
LAO TZU

In this chapter we will explore the different types of intuition. In the earlier discussion about intuition and psychology, we drew on the work of Assagioli who spoke of sensory intuitions being associated with conscious perceptions. Modern writers in the area have proposed a number of different sensory types of intuition; we will consider some of these so that you can identify which particular type(s) you relate to the most.

VISUAL, AUDITORY AND KINAESTHETIC SENSES

I have studied and practised many different models of therapy over the years, including hypnotherapy and Neuro-Linguistic Programming (NLP). Each of these models considers the ways in which we perceive events. NLP explores both perception and communication, explaining that we receive information from around us via our senses; that is, what we see (visual), hear (auditory), smell (olfactory), taste (gustatory) and feel (kinaesthetic). Our brain then assimilates this information and forms 'internal representations' of the events, which are also influenced by language and society.[1] NLP techniques can assist us in improving communication.

I first studied hypnotherapy twenty years ago and immediately felt a passion for it. Since then it has become an integral part of my professional work. Hypnosis involves a focusing of attention leading to an altered state of consciousness, different from sleep or the awake state. This is evident in the altered brain wave patterns; in the awake state there are beta waves, in early relaxation there are alpha waves, and in deeper relaxation (tranquil, creative) there are theta waves. In sleep we experience theta and delta waves. Hypnosis is characterised by various phenomena such as suggestibility (being open to hypnotic suggestion), time distortion (time seeming shorter or longer than in reality) and amnesia (forgetting the experience or part of it).[2]

Hypnosis is a similar state to meditation, but hypnotherapy can be differentiated by its use of suggestions and its role in managing clinical problems. The use of a sleep-like state has been recorded from ancient times, and in many cultures throughout the world shamans and healers use the power of words and ritual to heal.[3] When beginning hypnotherapy with an individual, it is important to work out whether they primarily use visual or other senses in their imagination to think and to relax. The therapist then incorporates these senses as part of the hypnotic deepening techniques, such as visualising a beautiful and relaxing beach, in order to maximise the effectiveness of the therapy.

It's equally important to establish our sensory preferences

when working with our intuition. To illustrate our tendencies towards one sense over another, I will draw on my own family. My sister is a dentist and a very skilled artist; she is very visual. This has been useful in both her profession and her art. She can picture her artistic creations in her mind before they appear on canvas and drawing is relaxing for her. My son has a strong auditory sense and, as a result, he is a good communicator and musician. His passion is music, so much so that when he was about ten years old and in primary school he represented his school house with a talk on how music had transformed his life. He has gone on to enjoy playing, performing and composing music. He also has a strong kinaesthetic sense and enjoys the feeling of playing and expressing emotions in the playing. Other examples of kinaesthetic activities are dance, jogging, surfing and touch.

Most individuals utilise a range of modalities, such as visual and auditory or auditory and kinaesthetic.[4] There is nothing I like more than walking on the beach (kinaesthetic), enjoying the sights and sounds (visual and auditory) and contemplating life. Recently someone said to me that that walking on the beach is their number one choice to relax, but their partner likes to watch nature shows on television. They could not understand how this could be relaxing. I explained that their partner is probably quite visual and probably relating to nature when he watches the documentaries, which can be very relaxing. To determine which modalities you relate to and use in your imagination or to relax, consider the following exercises. They will give you an indication of the different modalities (visual, auditory or kinaesthetic) you utilise.

Your senses

In your journal, answer the following questions:

1. How do you like to relax?
2. If you contemplate your last holiday in your mind, do you see images of it, hear sounds or feel yourself doing things?

In this book, a number of meditations will be provided. They are not only relaxing, but will help you to learn about yourself and are geared towards enhancing intuition. Meditation is a state of relaxation created by focusing attention and quietening the mind.[5] You may already have experience with meditation, but if not, it is important to be aware of some general guidelines. A good starting position for meditation is sitting in a chair with feet on the floor and hands on your lap or on the arms of the chair. Alternatively you can lie down if that is more comfortable. Choose a place to meditate that you associate with good feelings and try to ensure you will not be interrupted during your meditation. Make sure that the room is neither too hot nor too cold, wear comfortable clothing, remove your glasses if you want and dim the lights. Once you are set, use the following brief meditation. While it will be relaxing, it should also provide information about which senses you relate to the most.

FIRST SENSORY MEDITATION

Make yourself comfortable. If you are happy to close your eyes, then let them close. When you use the meditations in this book, you will always feel peaceful and safe.

Imagine that you are walking down a street near where you live. As you walk along, feel the ground under your feet and the sunshine on your body. Notice what you can see as you walk along — any houses or shops along the way. Notice too the plants and gardens, any cars parked at the side of the street, any post boxes or passers-by. Can you hear traffic or birds? As you stroll along, can you smell the flowers or feel the sunshine on your face or the gentle breeze?

You come across a tree with ripe fruit on it hanging over a fence. You stop to smell the fruit, and if you feel like it, you can pick a piece and taste it. Enjoy the scene with all of your senses then, when you are ready, open your eyes.

After the meditation, consider what you could see, hear, feel, taste or smell, as this will provide additional information. So far in this chapter, which senses are dominant for you? Is there a mix?

OUR SENSES AND INTUITION

Why the focus on sensations? Well, our senses are very important, as intuitive information initially comes to us through them.

Intuition is a blend of our five senses, and also involves our life experiences and values.[6] We mostly become aware of intuition via our vision, hearing and kinaesthetic sense, and at first one of these senses may dominate. As it is likely that we will have stronger capacities in one or two of these areas, we are going to explore each of these in more detail. One of the senses may be dominant, but do not worry if you are not strongly pulled to one area or another. Sometimes we have mixed perception! The text and tables that follow are based on the work of Penney Peirce and Lauren Thibodeau, who conduct training internationally on the subject of intuition.[7, 8]

Most people take in the majority of their information visually. Visual people love colour, learn by reading or may see images in their mind's eye. When they recall events, visual people see them as pictures. In the same way, intuition can be experienced predominantly visually, such as through flashes of colour or images in your daily life, in meditation or in dreams.[9, 10] To understand how strong your visual sense is in general as well as specifically in relation to intuition, consider the following questions. The more 'yes' responses that you have, the more visual you are likely to be.

Do you use your visual sense?

Consider the following questions and, in your journal, answer each one with either 'Yes', 'No' or 'Not Sure'.

1. Do you make a decision to purchase something based on how it looks?
2. Do you have a good sense of colour?
3. Do you remember faces rather than names?

4. Do you use phrases such as, 'I can see what you mean'?
5. Have you ever had an image in your mind of a friend before you unexpectedly met them?
6. Have you had a déjà vu experience, a sense that you have seen it all before?

Individuals who have a strong auditory sense often love chatting or music. They learn by listening or reading out loud, or they might remember names and conversations well. Auditory intuition may involve hearing a particular song with words that are meaningful to you at the time or a phrase coming up in a conversation that throws light on your current situation. Some people with auditory strengths are aware of an inner voice (inside their head) which is different to usual thoughts (perhaps calmer or of a different nature).[11] Has this sort of voice ever, for example, told you that you shouldn't go to an event and when you did go anyway someone there upset you? A few years ago, I had an interesting experience. I needed to move and when looking at a particular house, I heard an inner voice saying, 'This is more like it.' Interestingly, these were the sort of words my father would have used, not me! To understand how strongly you utilise your auditory sense, consider the following questions — the more 'Yes' responses, the more auditory you are likely to be.

Do you use your auditory sense?

Consider the following questions and, in your journal, answer each one with either 'Yes', 'No' or 'Not Sure'.

1. Do you love to talk or love music?

2. Are you good at languages?
3. Do you use phrases such as, 'It sounds like ... '?
4. Have you ever caught yourself humming a tune and then realised that the words of the song were the answer to a problem that had been troubling you?

The kinaesthetic sense involves feelings, touch or movement. Kinaesthetic individuals often like physical activities, such as dance or sport, and some like massage. They might find it important to have a comfortable couch in their lounge room. Sometimes intuition will be signalled kinaesthetically with skin tingling or goosebumps.[12] When I am talking about a new idea and I get goosebumps, then I know I am on to a good one! One night, when I was attending a meditation class run by my friend Heather, we decided to focus the meditation on our health. We began by talking about getting fit and trim, and somehow my grandfather — who was a talented footballer when he was young — came into the conversation, at which point we both experienced extremely strong goosebumps. Heather said, 'There's your answer. Your grandfather wants you to move more!'

Intuition may be signalled through feelings in the body; for example, picking up someone's health concerns empathically (feeling chest discomfort when with a smoker or someone with heart problems). Kinaesthetic intuition can be particularly strong in health professionals or healing practitioners. I have experienced it at times in my career, picking up on people's physical or emotional pain and feeling it in my body. Some individuals will have the experience of sensing someone is with them even though they may be far away or even deceased.[13, 14] To understand how strongly you utilise your kinaesthetic sense generally and intuitively, consider the following questions. The more 'Yes' responses you give, the more kinaesthetic you are likely to be.

Do you use your kinaesthetic sense?

Consider the following questions and, in your journal, answer each one with either 'Yes', 'No' or 'Not Sure'.

1. Do you enjoy sports or massage?
2. Do you often use the phrase, 'My sense is ...'?
3. When you tap into your memories, do you re-experience the associated feelings?
4. Do you sometimes sense when someone comes into the room even if they don't make a sound?
5. Do you get goosebumps at times, when an idea seems to be spot on?
6. Do certain people make you uncomfortable when you first meet them, even before they have said a word?
7. Do you sometimes feel pain in your body when someone else is in pain or unwell?

Hopefully, having explored the senses in more detail, you feel more confident about which sense or senses you are tapping into in your day-to-day life and intuitively. One may be dominant or you may feel there is a mix. Remember, there are no right or wrong answers in this book! Based on your responses to the exercises, do you primarily tap into your visual, auditory or kinaesthetic senses, or do you use a mix of all three? Are your olfactory (smell) or gustatory (taste) senses particularly important for you? Your answers will give you direction about which senses to pay more attention to or develop further.

MENTAL, EMOTIONAL AND KINAESTHETIC INTUITION

Modern-day authors on intuition have suggested a range of intuition styles. While there is some overlap between them, I think the work of counsellor and teacher Nancy Rosanoff is worth considering. She suggests that there are three primary ways intuition speaks to us, namely:

- Mental intuition or something like thoughts or hunches, which utilise our vision and other senses.
- Emotional, such as something feeling okay or not okay, or possibly picking up on other people's feelings, utilising our feelings and senses.
- Kinaesthetic, where physical feelings convey information, such as a gut-feeling or feeling in the chest, utilising kinaesthetic and other senses.

Rosanoff also comments that as intuition is not necessarily verbal or logical, we need to become sensitive to more subtle information, such as signs or symbols, feelings or physical sensations.[15]

Can you relate to these descriptions? Remember that we may experience a combination of all three styles. I have certainly experienced hunches and gut-feelings, including the feeling that something is okay or not okay, or that an individual is trustworthy or not. In my work, I focus on picking up on other people's emotions and often notice their impact on how I am feeling. Being a doctor, I have had many experiences of picking up on an individual's health concerns through feeling a pain in a particular area of my body. This can be both helpful and disconcerting — I'll be talking with a client and then experience chest pain. I have to realise who the pain belongs to and go from there! Have you ever had Reiki or another form of energy healing? The healer will often pick up on pain or illness in the body.

The following meditation set in a beautiful cottage and garden brings together some of these ideas. I cannot help but think about my beautiful cottage located about an hour down the coast. Originally a railway worker's cottage, it is over one hundred years old. My parents established a wonderful garden, full of fruit trees and old roses. Friends have named it the 'secret garden', and I now see it as my own secret garden; when you are in it, nothing else seems to exist.

SECOND SENSORY MEDITATION: THE COTTAGE AND GARDEN

Sit comfortably and allow your eyes to close. Relax more deeply as you imagine a path that leads to the front gate of a two-storey cottage. Feel the path under your feet and the sunshine on your face. There is a wooden gate that opens into a pretty cottage garden with flowers on either side of the path. Notice what you can see, hear, touch or smell in the garden.

Then enter the house through the blue front door. It leads into a welcoming entrance hall with a hall stand. You might like to hang up your coat. Do you feel the house welcoming you? There is a room on the left, a sitting room with a comfortable couch with striped upholstery, with light coming through the window. Notice all that you can see in the room and how comfortable the couch feels. What thoughts or feelings come into your mind?

There is another room on the other side of the hall. It has a stereo with all the music that you like available — you can sit there to listen to and enjoy the music. When you are finished there, go out to the kitchen. There is the smell of delicious cooking — what's in the oven? Take some time to smell and taste the food. What memories come to mind? What emotions are stirred?

Up the small staircase there is a bedroom with a comfortable bed, a thick quilt and lovely pillows to lie down on and have a rest. How does it feel to lie there? Is it incredibly comfortable? Do you dream for a moment?

When you are ready, return downstairs and explore the garden. There are many plants and flowers and corners of the garden to explore. There is a surprise for you in one corner — maybe a lovely fountain or a favourite flower. Enjoy the cottage and garden and, when you're ready, come back to the here and now.

I hope that you enjoyed the meditation. Spend a few moments reflecting on what you saw, heard, smelt, touched or felt in the cottage. Again, which senses dominated, and were there any surprises?

TYPES OF INTUITION

- We receive information from around us via our senses (vision, hearing, smell, taste and feeling), and we may use a range of these.
- We might use mental intuition including thoughts or hunches, and involving vision, signs and symbols.
- We might use emotional intuition involving our feelings and senses, or physical or kinaesthetic intuition from bodily feelings.

REFLECTIONS

We can learn such a lot from our sensations and experiences. Being more familiar with your intuitive type(s) will help you to focus on particular sensations when you are doing some of the exercises later in the book. Tapping into the different sensations that are strong for you will help you to relax more deeply, and will assist you in recognising your intuitive experiences in your everyday life. In coming days, focus on being more aware of the information you are receiving through your senses and, in particular, to any intuitive information, perhaps via thoughts or feelings.

Your 'intuition garden' journal

In your journal, write down your answers to the following questions:

1. What have you learnt about yourself in this chapter?
2. Note any other reflections.

Chapter 4

THE SEVEN STEPS
TO INTUITION

The journey of a thousand miles begins with one step.
LAO TZU

This chapter is the cornerstone to the book and to enhancing your intuition. It is built around the two key areas mentioned at the start of this section, namely developing the different levels of intuition and building your relationship with self and your inner knowing, and with others. It is based too on the idea that we can enhance our intuition through training. There is a great deal written now about training the mind and we can certainly undertake intuition training.[1, 2] After all, intuition is an innate ability and the mind is capable of ongoing change and development throughout our lifetimes.

Many of the themes from the first section of the book in relation to developing your intuition have contributed to the seven steps that I describe in this chapter. These themes are reviewed below:

- Different levels of intuition have been proposed relating to the conscious and unconscious levels of the mind, and potentially a 'Higher Self' or inner wisdom.

- Intuition can act like a compass to guide us in life.
- Mindfulness involves paying purposeful attention to the present and it activates nerve cell growth.
- We are likely to use our intuition when we are in a positive mood and rested. In sleep we tap into creative and intuitive functions of our brain.
- Empathy, creativity and intuition are housed in the same area of the brain.
- We can be taught intuition, through journalling, mapping decision-making, getting feedback on intuitive decisions and using relaxation.
- We often move backwards and forwards between rational thinking and intuition in decision-making.
- Symbols and dreams can be keys to our unconscious emotional life.

Let's also review and incorporate some of the ideas that came out of interviewing people for the book. I was fortunate to be able to speak with a number of people who had worked on enhancing their intuition. Themes that came out of these interviews were the value of slowing life down, reading, undertaking courses, meditation, journal writing, creative or spiritual pursuits and self-reflection. Life experience (positive and suffering) played a valuable part. Some of the interview highlights were:

Natalie said that she has developed her intuition through reading and doing a short course on developing intuition. The course demystified intuition, encouraged careful observation of people and fostered trust in gut-feelings. Her own experiences of grief were influential too.

Liz said that her life experiences had taught her most about her intuition and that prayer had assisted.

Melanie realised in recent years that you could develop your intuition further and had become more aware through reading and attending a meditation group.

Lynn found that her art therapy training assisted, as well as other courses related to healing that she has attended.

Sandy said that in some parts of her life intuition had functioned well for many years, such as in relationships with those close to her, particularly her mother and, interestingly, in cooking! Living her life and growing in experience led her to accept that intuition has an important role in and impact on how to lead her life.

Gia has found that meditation (alone or in a group), massage and bodywork, journal writing, drawing/mandala work, prayer, yoga, angel cards, walks on the beach or in the hills, travel, self-reflection, slowing life down, creative activities (singing, dance, acting) and detoxing have all assisted her to be in touch with her intuition.

I have created a series of steps designed to assist you in developing your intuition. It is likely that, as we are individuals, some of the ideas presented in each step will be a fit for you but not all. You are the expert on yourself and your own intuition, so I suggest that you explore the ideas and adapt them for yourself. It is by practising the skills highlighted in each step that you will further develop your intuition. Morita, a Japanese therapist, refers to effort as being 'good fortune';[3] and the Buddha spoke of the Noble Eightfold Path, which included right intention, right action and right effort. So the more you practise, the greater your sense of mastery and confidence in your new skills.

THE SEVEN STEP MODEL OF INTUITION

The seven steps to grow your intuition form the framework for the remainder of this chapter. A visual model of these steps appears below — note what sits at the centre of them all! We will now look at each step in detail and you'll find there are a number of exercises for you to practise or complete.

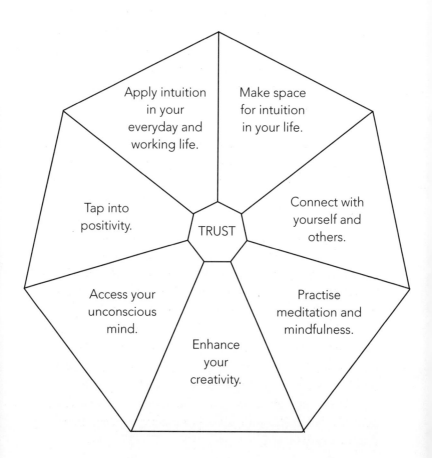

STEP 1: MAKE SPACE FOR INTUITION IN YOUR LIFE

When establishing a garden, you usually reach a stage when you need to do some clearing out to make space for your garden ideas. You clear weeds and old plants to make way for the new plantings. You prepare the soil, adding compost and digging holes in which to plant the new plants, and prepare the space for any features. In the same way, when we work on developing our intuition, we need to clear the mind at the outset and make space for intuition in our lives. This is especially relevant in our busy and stimulating lives.

DE-CLUTTERING OUR MIND AND LIVES

De-cluttering refers to clearing out what is no longer useful. It can refer to de-cluttering objects, aspects of our life or our minds. As a child, I always enjoyed sorting out my room, clearing out any no longer needed items and making way for the new. Even as an adult I still enjoy rearranging the furniture in my house and having a spring clean. My son seems to share this interest: at five years of age he informed his surprised headmistress that his favourite activity was rearranging his room! When we moved house a year ago, he spent the first few hours putting up posters and photos in his room, stamping his identity and experiencing joy in finding a place for each of his belongings.

However, even though I knew that I always enjoyed de-cluttering at home or the office, and liked the sense of order and a fresh start that followed, I had not really paid attention to all the potential benefits of de-cluttering until quite recently when my friend Heather spoke to me over coffee one day about its wider benefits. She pointed out that it seems to not only refresh the space but also to re-energise us. Perhaps this is due to the exercise involved and the focusing of our attention on a task, but maybe there is more to it. Subsequently, I am now more aware that after a good de-clutter my energy is renewed and I feel less weighed down by the old. In addition, things in life often seem to then rearrange themselves — perhaps new ideas or opportunities arise! It's certainly an interesting phenomenon.

We live in a world full of material things and every day we are surrounded by advertising and opportunities to increase the amount of belongings in our lives. Sometimes we need to think about this and set our own boundaries for how much 'stuff' we will allow to enter our lives, our homes and workspaces. My mother once heard an elderly psychiatrist on the radio saying that as we get older we should gradually reduce our material belongings. He was retired and had downsized to live in a caravan with just a few belongings. It's good to have regular clean-outs of our houses, offices and cars. Put the music on and enjoy the experience! Are there items related to projects you haven't and probably won't complete? Could someone else make use of them? Unwanted goods can be donated to charity or you can have a garage sale. It's important, however, to hold onto things that give you joy or that have nice memories attached.

But how does all of this relate to intuition? Well, my experience is that when the mind is overloaded or 'cluttered' (and perhaps too fatigued or overstimulated), it is very difficult to get in touch with our intuition. Peirce refers to 'creating a clear lens' as being an early step in the process and I see de-cluttering as part of this. So making space for intuition in your life may involve de-cluttering the diary so that you are less stressed and fatigued, and allowing time for relaxation and meditation instead.

Reflect on how you can make more space for intuition in your life by trying the following meditation.

THE SINGLE BOX MEDITATION
FOR CLUTTER-CLEARING

Make yourself comfortable and let your eyes close. Focus on your breath and relax a little more with each breath out.

In your mind's eye visualise a box. It may be made out of timber or cardboard, it may be large or small, decorated or plain. Whatever comes to mind is just right for you. If visualising does not come readily, that's fine; use your other senses to get in touch with your box.

This is a very special box. Into this box you can place any clutter from your life that you wish to clear. Maybe you want to clear excess belongings or 'stuff', maybe stress and worry, or maybe you can use this box to get a sense of clearing other aspects of your life. This will help you to make space for other things, including your intuition. Put whatever you need to into the box and get in touch with the feeling of making space in your life for intuition. Spend as long as you want doing this. Then, when you are ready, open your eyes and come back to the room.

SELF-CARE

How mindful are you of caring for yourself? Do you put others before yourself? Are you low down on your priority list? Do you eat well, get enough sleep, spend time relaxing and exercising?

Sonia Choquette, an author and spiritual teacher, advises that self-care is necessary to be able to be intuitive. We learnt earlier that sleep and intuitive abilities are connected. When did you last have a sleep-in, catch up with a friend, take a bike ride, go on a walk, or enjoy a long relaxing bath? Choquette suggests that an Epsom salt bath (or any salt) is a great way to not only look after yourself but also clear your own energy.[4] I regularly enjoy a bath with salts after a long day at work and find it very therapeutic.

Self-care plan

In your journal, answer the following questions:
1. How can you take better care of yourself in the coming months?
2. What needs to change?

DE-CLUTTER YOUR OLD STORIES!

Another aspect to de-cluttering is ridding our lives of any 'old story' that is holding us back. Choquette recommends appreciating the old story, writing it down, telling it, noticing how you feel in relation to it, and then letting it go.[5] Stories feature in a number of different psychotherapies but in particular in narrative therapy. This therapy is based on the idea that stories are made up of events that we link together across a time period in a way that makes sense to us. These stories make the daily events of our lives meaningful.[6] We have lots of stories about our lives; for example, about ourselves, our abilities, our struggles, our work, our dreams and our relationships. We link them together and give them meaning, such as 'I'm a good mother'. At times, they may be negative stories. We can create a powerful story about ourselves called 'Who I am', but remember that no single story can completely cover all aspects of our life.[7]

If we have some negative stories dominating our lives (such as 'I'm not worthy'), narrative therapy can help us to think differently about ourselves. It invites us to consider the following questions and, in doing so, to think differently:

- Can you identify one of the stories about yourself?
- How has it impacted on your view of yourself?
- Have there been times when in some small way you have been able to stand up to this story and stopped it pushing you around?
- What qualities or abilities did it take for you to resist the story?[8]

Narrative therapy

You might like to work through the questions listed above in your journal. Write down your responses and reflect on how you might view yourself in a different way.

- We need to clear the mind and make space for intuition in our lives.
- De-cluttering refers to clearing out what is no longer useful.
- De-clutter the diary to reduce stress and allow time for relaxation and meditation.
- Clear some space to take care of yourself to enhance your intuition.
- De-cluttering can refer to clearing our lives of any unhelpful 'old stories'.

STEP 2:
CONNECT WITH YOURSELF
AND OTHERS

To be intuitive, we need to not only make space in our lives and our minds but we also need to know ourselves better and connect with others. Steiner said that to develop our inner knowing 'we should periodically turn and look inward, shaping our basic principles of life, mentally reviewing what we know'.[9] He also wrote about the importance of achieving a sense of balance or serenity in life.[10] And as we mentioned earlier, Saint Teresa of Avila wrote of the importance of self-knowledge in our spiritual journey. Thus an important aspect of becoming more intuitive is having a deeper relationship with your inner self and your inner knowing, as well as with others.

In this step you will be invited to identify your values

and set some goals (including goals related to your personal development, your intuition and relationships). We will also look at ways to continue to enhance your self-awareness and knowledge. Connecting with and balancing the body, mind and spirit, and developing your empathy skills are all essential.

IDENTIFY YOUR VALUES AND SET SOME GOALS

If you want to live a satisfying and fulfilling life or want to make changes such as enhancing your intuition, a good starting point is considering what is important to you in life. What do you truly value? One of the other therapies that I utilise is Acceptance and Commitment Therapy (ACT). This behavioural therapy, which draws on Eastern philosophies, talks about different areas or domains in life, namely:

- family and friends
- romance or intimate relationships
- health and your body
- education and personal development
- work and finance
- leisure and creativity
- citizenship or community life (from using the local library to volunteering)
- environment or nature
- spirituality.[11]

Let's incorporate intuition into this list! It might come under the personal development area for you or you might relate to it in the spirituality domain. Now consider your values in relation to each of these domains. What is important to you in each of these areas? For example, under the heading of work, having a satisfying job might be important. Under leisure, you might value playing sport, catching up with friends or going to craft classes. Under personal development, you might value going to courses or working through books such as this one! It's time to explore this in more detail.

Personal values

In your journal, draw up a table that looks like the one following. Take time to consider your values as you complete it.

Life domains (include intuition in one of these areas)	What are my values in each of these areas?	Is there a gap between what I value and what is happening now?
Family, friends and other relationships		
Romance or intimate relationships		
Health and your body		
Education and personal development (intuition?)		
Work and finance		
Leisure and creativity		
Citizenship or community life		
Environment or nature		
Spirituality (intuition?)		

Life domains	Goals	Timeframe	I will know that I have achieved this goal when ...
e.g. Leisure	Engage in my leisure activities more often, for about an hour at a time, several times a week, over the next 3 months	3 months	I will journal my leisure activities and record how long I spend on them.

You can then develop your goals by looking at areas where there are gaps between what is important to you and what is happening at present; for example, you might value a satisfying job but you might not perceive your current work as being satisfying. You might also value your intuition but have been too busy recently to have much experience of it.

The next exercise will assist you to set your goals. Remember that goals need to be *owned* by you, they need to be specific and have a timeframe attached to them; for example, 'I will work on my intuition over the next twelve months, by making some time to read about intuition and creating a space at home to practise meditation or intuition exercises three times a week. I will know when I have achieved this goal when I have practised regularly and am noticing my intuition more often.'

Personal goals

In your journal, draw up a table similar to the one on the next page. Take your time completing it.

CONNECT WITH YOUR BODY, MIND AND SPIRIT

We are made up of body, mind and spirit. Connecting with each of these is vital to our wellbeing and to our intuition. When considering body, mind and spirit, which one are you most comfortable with? Do you feel grounded in your body and enjoy movement or do you seem to spend more time in your mind, thinking or expressing yourself verbally? Or are you a visionary, feeling inspired or 'not of this world' (spirit)?[12] You may find you're more in touch with one than another.

You can learn more about this by thinking about what you avoid. For example, you might feel uncomfortable with your body and avoid physical activities. Or you might avoid being quiet because you're worried that you will get caught up in your thinking or emotions. As a result you may stay physically very busy instead. Perhaps you do not have a sense of spirit in your life, the essence of who you are or a sense of Higher Self. You might want to re-focus your attention onto an area that you are avoiding. Or if you are uncomfortable with one area, you might choose to combine areas; for example, doing something physical in a mental or spiritual way such as yoga or tai chi.[13]

It is said that in the Western world we spend a lot of time 'in our heads' rather than 'in our bodies'. This makes sense given that we do less physical work than in the past and spend a lot of time with technology. So let's consider the body for a moment. Do you like your body, do you exercise your body and do you honour your body? When we are busy looking after children or working, often the body is low down on the priority list. Healthy eating and exercise may fall away. Consider getting more in touch with your body by moving it through exercise, walking on beach sand, having a massage and eating lots of colourful foods, like fruit and vegetables. Take time each day to notice how your body feels. Is there tension anywhere? What sensations are occurring?

It we think back to the different types of intuition, it stands to reason that being more aware of your body will allow you to pick up on kinaesthetic sensations such as gut-feelings, goosebumps or feeling pulled in a particular direction. With intuition, it's important to feel grounded or connected to the earth, and related to this is feeling connected to your body. I have to constantly work on this connection as I am often very busy. Finding time to walk the dogs or have a spa or massage helps a great deal. I also find there is nothing better than going to the markets and buying fresh produce, cooking it up that night and fuelling my body with nutritious food.

I can remember an occasion when my body provided me with some really interesting information. After I wrote my first book, an organisation approached me saying that they were very interested in publishing my work and making it available to the Australian market. I thought this would be worthwhile and had talks with them. At one of the talks, an advisor to the organisation was there who sat with crossed arms and looking away from me. It didn't take much skill to observe that he was not interested in my work. He only spoke once and that was about a program that *he* was developing.

I was asked to write up a formal proposal, but on the day that it was to be considered by the organisation's board of management I felt shaky and unwell. During the afternoon I had uncomfortable sensations in my back. When the call came late in the afternoon that the board had said 'no' to my book, I realised what the sensations were about! The experience was very disappointing but I learnt from it. I decided to look beyond this organisation and to take a chance and send the book to a British publisher. It was accepted and enabled me to get my work out to a much larger audience, and this gave me the confidence to write more books!

It is just as important to connect with your mind by being aware of your thoughts and feelings, and to connect with your spirit, or the essence of you, your energy, your uniqueness. I have studied or worked with people for 30 years now and I am constantly amazed by their stories and resilience. Despite adversity, their mind and spirit often shine through. I am not often moved to tears with a client but recently an older woman shared her life story and I cried with her. Despite the many challenges she had faced, she had not only survived but thrived, thinking positively and leading an active life in the community and gaining great pleasure from helping others. I have also been with individuals when they are dying, and at the time of death I receive a strong sense of their spirit as opposed to the physical body that remains.

Getting in touch with your sense of spirit

In your journal, answer the following questions about yourself.
1. What do you feel passionate about?
2. What gives you joy?

Now try the following meditation to assist in connecting with your spirit.

MEDITATION ON SPIRIT

Make yourself comfortable and let your eyes close. Focus on the breath and relax a little more with each breath out. Reflect on a time when you felt connected with your essence or spirit. When was it? What were you doing? Where were you? How did it feel? Get in touch with those feelings and enjoy them. Take time to feel the passion, feel the joy. Then take these feelings into the heart and hold them there. Does a particular colour come to mind in relation to those feelings? Now let those feelings or the colour spread through the entire body and mind. You have amazing spirit. Let it shine through every day. When you want to, return your focus of attention to sounds in the room, have a stretch and open your eyes.

BALANCE BODY, MIND AND SPIRIT

One of my goals is to achieve a greater sense of balance between body, mind and spirit. I have to admit that I struggle with this, as not only is life busy and demanding, but I tend to take on a lot! In his book *Perfect Balance*, Paul Wilson speaks of imbalance occurring when there is conflict between the things we have to do, should do, things others want us to do, and things we want to do.[14] I can certainly relate to this. At one time I asked a group of health professionals I was teaching, 'What does balance mean to you?' They responded with 'Paying attention to all areas [or domains] in life' — so very true. It's important to remember that 'balance' is not a static concept; it is a bit like a ladybird that will settle on you for a while and then fly away again.

One of my favourite films is *Eat Pray Love*. In the film, based on the book of the same name, the protagonist takes a year-long journey to Italy, India and Bali to search for a sense of self and balance. But as the Balinese healer, Ketut, says towards the end of the film, sometimes living a balanced life means being out of balance at times! The aim is to achieve regular periods of balance in life, to help achieve a sense of harmony between body, mind and spirit, and a sense of wellbeing. This is important because when we are more rested and feeling a sense of balance, we are more likely to be in tune with our senses and our inner knowing.

One key aspect of finding balance is making sure to remember the simple things in life. It was the Roman Emperor Marcus Aurelius who apparently said, 'Very little is needed to make a happy life.' Some of the best things in life, like the beauty of nature or a child's smile, can be overlooked in our very materialistic world. A client once said, 'When I started enjoying the simple things again, I knew I was getting over the depression.' The ritual of making a good cup of tea or picking some flowers from the garden can provide a lot of pleasure. Sometimes we keep searching for the 'thing' that will provide happiness in life, rather than looking at what we already have. How often do we think, 'I'll be happy when ... ', rather than focusing on the now.

My mother died not that long ago. She instilled in me the message of finding joy and experiencing beauty in the simple things in life. As I write this section, it is Christmas and I know that she wanted to be mentioned in this book. To honour this wish, and in honour of her philosophy, I am writing about her right now! In fact, I was reminded (was this synchronicity?)

of her philosophy when I came across a little book recently by lifestyle writer Leigh Crandall called *A Book of Simple Pleasures*. It speaks of there being a lot going on in our lives at present and suggests that we return to elementary pleasures.[15] Both my mother and father found enormous pleasure in their garden and its many roses and they created a haven. Mum loved baking, sewing and reading and could always amuse herself. This is an art. Hence, this book had to go into my Christmas stocking from Mum, as a reminder of her message to fill your life with little pleasures, focus on the moment and enjoy those pleasures!

Simple pleasures

Consider which simple pleasures you enjoy, and how you might incorporate more of these into your life. If you would like to, jot down your thoughts in your journal.

ENHANCE YOUR SELF-AWARENESS

Self-awareness refers to getting to know and accept yourself more fully, reviewing your ideas, and being open to new information and experiences.[16] We can develop our self-awareness through noticing our internal state, mood and thoughts, by reading books, watching films or documentaries, talking with others, journalling, meditation, reflection or prayer, travelling, personal development courses, further study, creative activities, being in touch with nature (for example, gardening or walking in a park or at the beach), or undertaking psychotherapy. Many of the exercises in this book are aimed at developing your self-awareness and self-acceptance, as these will enhance your intuition. By using your journal to write down your reflections and observations, you will raise your self-awareness.

Sometimes feelings or thoughts just pop into our awareness in an instant, sometimes described as 'a flash', and perhaps only lasting a moment. I can recall a number of these. One experience relates to a time as a teenager when I somehow knew that a friend who had been travelling for about eighteen months was back in Australia. I had a flash of intuition that she was back and rang her mother. Her surprised mother said that she had come back earlier than anticipated and was asleep, recovering from jetlag. I went to visit my friend the next day to catch up on her trip and she was bemused at how I could have known she was back. I couldn't readily explain it at the time either. Only recently, I was talking with a client about her dream house. Immediately I pictured a two-storey house overlooking the beach. She went on to say that this was her dream and she enjoyed my being able to picture it with her.

Another example in my family occurred when my mother was near the end of her life and often unwell with infections. I would visit more often at these times, never knowing whether that particular infection would lead to her final decline. On one occasion I had had a very busy week and was extremely tired but had to fly out at lunchtime that day to teach interstate for the weekend. I got up at 7 a.m. to go in early to visit my mother. When I went to say goodbye to my son, he said to me, 'You don't need to go Mum, don't go.' Sensing that he had had a flash of intuition, I responded, 'Is it about Nan?' He said, 'Nan is fine. It's about you. Don't go.' I listened to him and visited my mother after my trip instead. Mum was fine. I don't know what might have happened had I visited, but I do know that I was very tired and that trying to squeeze in another visit would perhaps not necessarily have been a safe idea.

Increased self-awareness is often the outcome of therapy, whether in the form of learning more about our thinking styles, our emotional life, how we relate to others or how to manage behaviours. As I mentioned earlier, I practise multimodal therapy, incorporating a range of approaches, with the underlying aim being to take a holistic approach, addressing all areas in life including the spiritual if appropriate. Sometimes we hesitate to go there, but a client with Christian beliefs recently thanked me for incorporating discussion about her faith and how prayer could assist her recovery. If others have a Buddhist philosophy, then we may talk about Buddhist principles; if they believe in angels, then we refer to angels. I am passionate about exploring all of these philosophies or approaches, as understanding them helps me to relate to individuals with a diverse range of beliefs.

Abraham Maslow, a psychologist who studied healthy people in the 1960s, developed the concept of 'self-actualisaton'. This involves experiencing things fully, listening to yourself, using your intelligence and finding out who you are and what your mission is. He saw this process as requiring courage. Psychosynthesis, as discussed in the first chapter, aims to assist the individual to know themselves in a holistic way and speaks of awakening our ability to be guided by 'Self'. And some of the reasons that I practise hypnotherapy are that it can assist individuals to get in touch with a sense of Self or inner wisdom as well as lending itself to a holistic approach.

I have used the following exercise in practice for many years, either in discussion or as a visualisation. I originally came across a version of it, using boxes, in a book on hypnosis by Marlene

Hunter and over the years I have adapted the metaphor in a number of different ways.[17] The exercise involves imagining three buckets with lids. Years ago, a friend decoupaged three boxes for me as a gift, and they have sat in my office for many years assisting with my explanation of this metaphor. Recently I added three small plastic wheelie bins as props for the exercise. They're a hit! So why not try the meditation for yourself?

THE THREE BUCKET MEDITATION

Make yourself comfortable and let your eyes close. Now imagine three buckets with lids, sitting on a shelf. Notice the size and colours of the buckets. The first bucket represents everything to do with you and your life — your dreams and goals, ideas, intuition and interests. The second bucket represents other people and everything to do with them. The third bucket represents the world we live in, the social codes we live by (laws, morals) and the environment.

Lift the lid off the first bucket and take a look inside. You can spend a lot of time dealing with everything in this bucket and you can influence it greatly. You can work on your goals and intuition or remove things from this bucket.

Now have a look in the second bucket, to do with other people. You can influence this bucket to some degree, by helping or hindering, and you can learn a lot from it. But you have less control over this bucket and sometimes you need to put the lid on this bucket and put it back on the shelf.

Now explore the third bucket. Again, you can add to this bucket by getting involved with your community or by helping the environment, but there might be limits to what you can do.

Sometimes we need to focus on our own bucket and put the others aside for a while. This can help us to increase our self-awareness.

When you are ready, open your eyes and come back to the room.

Sometimes we need to allow time and space for reflection, perhaps sitting quietly at home, in the garden, while walking at the beach or meditating. Other individuals like to journal their thoughts, perhaps even posing a question and responding either then or later. In the past couple of years I have worked with international author and therapist, the Rev. Dr Stephanie Dowrick. She has written a wonderful book on creative journalling and at one point suggests that journalling is helpful in bringing together the functions of the left and right sides of the brain: 'One minute you are writing something about your day that is useful to remember (left brain), then suddenly you are off, making an association that takes you in an unexpected direction (right brain).' She suggests that you write down a problem that you want to solve and which you are prepared to leave for a day or two, and then come back to it later. In the meantime, your unconscious will have solved it for you.[18]

Shakti Gawain, an author and spiritual teacher, has written many books over the years and recorded CDs on creative visualisation and meditation. One, called *Developing Intuition*, contains a number of excellent meditations. I have adapted one of them here.[19] It relates to recalling a time when we experienced intuition.

AWARENESS OF INTUITION MEDITATION

Make yourself comfortable in a quiet spot, and let your eyes close. Breathe gently in and out, and focus all of your attention on the breath. Allow each breath to relax you more deeply. Feeling peaceful and safe, recall a time when you experienced intuition in your life, maybe a gut-feeling or a hunch. Allow your mind to recall such a time and notice how the intuition felt. Also notice what happened following this experience or didn't happen. Maybe you paid attention to it or maybe you dismissed it.

You might recall another time when you experienced intuition. What did you learn from this experience? Take your time and don't be concerned if something or nothing comes to mind. Sometimes it comes to mind now and sometimes later.

When you're ready, be aware of the breath again and your body and open your eyes, back in the here and now.

What did you notice in this meditation? To continue to work on self-awareness, Gawain suggests meditating for a few minutes and keeping a journal at the end of each day. Review the day in your mind, what you did and how you were feeling at the time. Notice any intuitive feelings or times when you felt 'in the flow'. This is a term sometimes used in literature about intuition, a sense of being right there in the moment, perhaps where you need to be or doing what you are meant to be doing. It can also refer to feeling 'in the flow' emotionally, at peace and content.[20]

If this section has resonated with you, it might be helpful

to pursue some individual therapy. Dealing with emotional concerns through your own self-development work or having some therapy can help you get to know yourself better and move forward in life. There are also books that can help you to deal with emotional issues at different times in your life. For example, Judith Orloff's book *Emotional Freedom* provides some very helpful techniques for working through a range of emotions, from fear to frustration. She focuses on building inner calm, connection with others, hope and compassion.[21]

CONNECT WITH OTHERS AND PRACTISE EMPATHY

We are social beings and relationships are central to our lives, whether they are with loved ones, friends, people in our community or co-workers. When you looked at your values, I wonder what you wrote about that was important to you in relation to others, such as support or friendship, and whether this was an area to work on further. Regularly connect with others and nurture your relationships. Remember too that often what we gain from a relationship reflects what we put into it. We were reminded earlier of how important empathy is in relating to others and in developing our intuition. The roots of empathy develop in our early years as we relate to caregivers and learn about empathy in play. Play is instinctive; in our early years it is in play that we tap into our imaginations and experience joy and creativity.[22] We continue to learn empathy as we relate to others in our families and at school, and as the brain matures.

Empathy is all about stepping into someone else's shoes or world and understanding their feelings or perspective. When we are empathic, we become attuned to others. Empathy involves paying attention to non-verbal cues from others, listening to what they are saying and reflecting on what we have heard and observed. We can be empathic in relation to both the content of what the person is saying and also their emotions. So practise empathy in your life. Focus outward, look and listen, and be aware of what you notice. Try feeding this back to others and they will soon tell you whether or not you are close. You will find it becomes easier with practice and your relationships will be enhanced. You will also find that you start having more hunches, are more tuned in to others' emotions, and will experience more kinaesthetic feelings.

CONNECT WITH YOURSELF AND OTHERS

- Consider your values in life and develop goals.
- Connect with your body, mind and spirit, and aim to achieve regular periods of balance.
- Enjoy the simple pleasures in life.
- To be intuitive, we need to know ourselves better and accept ourselves more fully.
- Notice feelings or thoughts that pop into your awareness.
- Reflection is important, such as in journalling or meditating on past intuition experiences.
- Empathy is about understanding others' feelings; with empathy, you are likely to have more hunches and to experience more kinaesthetic feelings.

STEP 3: PRACTISE MEDITATION AND MINDFULNESS

We need to find inner stillness to allow our intuition to come through and we can do this through meditation and mindfulness. These practices are to us like water to a garden. Meditation is a state of relaxation created by focusing attention and quietening the mind. Mindfulness stems from Buddhist and Hindu practices and refers to paying purposeful attention to the present moment.[23] There is everyday mindfulness (such as being in the present moment when doing simple activities such as having a bath or walking) as well as a range of specific mindfulness techniques. There are many benefits to the body's functioning from mindfulness meditation, including enhancing the immune response, dealing with stress and creating a sense of physical wellbeing.[24] This step will explore how meditation and mindfulness can help us to connect with our intuition.

MEDITATION

You will probably have heard more about meditation over the years than mindfulness. It is central to many Eastern spiritual practices but has become more common in the Western world since the 1960s. Most meditations involve focusing on the breath or tapping into your senses, through techniques such as visualisation, in order to achieve a state of focused concentration that calms the mind and body. As well as being relaxing, exercises such as these can also assist you to feel connected with nature, yourself and your intuition. It is important to get into the habit of meditating. Often we make excuses for not meditating — most commonly, 'I don't have time'

— but even a few minutes undertaken regularly will benefit you.

Several earlier meditations involved the senses; in this next one we focus on nature.

ENJOYING NATURE MEDITATION

Make yourself comfortable, let your eyes close, and imagine following a path to a lovely spot in nature, somewhere you enjoy and where you feel completely safe. You can be on your own or have someone with you. Some people like to imagine going to the beach or for a walk in the countryside. Connect with being in nature. Feel the ground under your feet and experience nature with all of your senses. Notice the colour of the sky, the fluffy clouds, a gentle breeze, the warmth of the sun and the fresh smell. Do you want to sit and enjoy what you can see or do you want to walk? What can you see around you, hear or touch?

Don't be concerned if you can't visualise very well. You might like to focus on one of your other senses that you relate to more. For example, you might like to listen to some music that you associate with nature or you might simply want to focus on feeling a deepening sense of relaxation and comfort in your body that you would experience out in nature.

Enjoy the surrounds and the pleasant feelings for as long as you like. When you are ready, gradually re-orient yourself to the present moment by being aware of the sounds around you, gently opening your eyes and looking around, and having a stretch.

We are all capable of practising meditation. It is important to not be too critical of yourself if thoughts come into your mind during meditation, as we all have busy minds. It's natural! Just notice the thoughts and let them pass, like clouds floating across the sky. Again effort is required in this area; that is, we improve our meditation with practice, even if we meditate for just a few minutes a day. Remember that it is important to choose a time when it is safe for you to practise and you can be undisturbed. Ensure that the setting is comfortable (temperature-wise, noise-wise and so on), and sit or lie down. A good place to start is by learning relaxation techniques. These can focus on the physical self, mental relaxation or a combination of both. Different people will be able to relax in different ways. Some individuals relax through visual means, such as reading, watching movies, looking at trees or the ocean. Some relax through the auditory sense, such as by listening to music, while others like to relax through the kinaesthetic sense with swimming or tai chi, for example. However, there are some basic meditation techniques that everyone can learn and enjoy, such as the breathing technique given on the next page.[25]

BREATHING MEDITATION

Make yourself comfortable and allow your eyes to close. Slow your breathing rate by closing your mouth and taking a breath in through your nose for a count of three, and then exhale the breath through your nose for a count of three. Repeat this breathing pattern.

Breathing through the nose helps most people to slow down their breathing naturally, but if you find it uncomfortable it is okay to breathe through your mouth.

It may be helpful to use a word to say to yourself in your mind as you exhale, such as 'relax', 'calm', 'peace' or whatever you find calming. And if you can, use abdominal breathing during this technique; that is, breathe down to your abdomen and allow it to expand as you breathe in. Spend a while focusing on the breath. When you are ready, be aware of sounds around you, be aware of the body, then open your eyes, back in the room.

MINDFULNESS

Jon Kabat-Zinn, who introduced mindfulness to Western psychology, talks about mindfulness as being a particular way of paying attention, on purpose and in the present moment.[26] We spend a lot of our time in 'mindlessness' or not paying attention. As a result we miss out on experiences in life and we can get caught up in ruminations about the past or worries about the future. Mindfulness has also been described as 'the non-judgmental observation of the ongoing stream of internal and external stimuli as they arise'.[27] Practising mindfulness involves being more observant, fully present and more connected to ourselves, others and the world. Through mindfulness we can learn that thoughts and feelings come and go, that we can have more balance and experience more peacefulness. It also develops self-acceptance and self-compassion.[28] Mindfulness involves paying attention to experience in the moment as opposed to being caught up in thoughts. It fosters an attitude of openness and curiosity. Even if our experience in the moment is difficult, we can be open to it instead of running from or fighting with it. In addition, mindfulness promotes flexibility: the ability to consciously direct our attention to different aspects of experience.[29]

The following meditation is an example of a simple mindfulness technique that anyone can use.[30]

MINDFULNESS MEDITATION

Make yourself comfortable and let your eyes close. Notice the chair or bed underneath you, supporting you, and notice the feel of your hands on your lap. Be aware of your breath, of the feel of the air as you breathe in and out, of breathing into the base of your lungs. Feel your abdomen rise and fall. Relax with each breath out.

Be aware of the body, of feelings of relaxation flowing from the feet upwards through the body, up through the legs, the back, the chest, the head and neck and down into the arms. Notice how the body feels as you relax. Sometimes it can feel a bit lighter or heavier. Sometimes it feels as if you could not move it even if you wanted to.

Now notice the sounds around you. Some are closer and some are further away. Focus on the sounds further away for a few moments. Now focus on the sounds closer to you. What can you hear? Again, bring your awareness to the feel of your body and the breath.

Have a gentle stretch. Then, when you are ready, open your eyes and be back in the room. Notice what is around you.

LABYRINTHS

Another fascinating way to meditate mindfully is walking a labyrinth. Labyrinths involve circular paths that move towards the centre of the circle and then out again. Walking them is very meditative. As you walk and focus on the path, you practise mindfulness, or some people use a mantra or prayer as they walk. You can also ask a question of yourself prior to the walk and then take some moments at the centre of the labyrinth to become aware of the answer. It was St Augustine who said, 'It is solved by walking.'[31] It's also possible to purchase handheld labyrinths that you can follow with your fingers, a much more portable form of labyrinth for meditation!

PRACTISE MEDITATION AND MINDFULNESS

- To nurture your intuition, find inner stillness through meditation and mindfulness.
- Meditation is a state of focused concentration that calms the mind and body.
- A good place to start when learning meditation is with relaxation techniques.
- Mindfulness refers to paying attention in the present moment. It involves tapping into your senses more fully and being more observant.
- Mindfulness helps us better connect to ourselves (our intuition), others and the world.
- Labryinths are meditative; we can meditate on a question as we walk.

STEP 4: ENHANCE YOUR CREATIVITY

While tapping into your creativity can enhance your intuition, it's equally true that tapping into your intuition can enhance your creativity! As Choquette writes, 'The highest, most joyful expression of the Spirit within comes through creativity. Nothing is more powerful. Nothing is more self-loving. It doesn't matter what you create, as long as it makes your life more beautiful and satisfying.'[32] In this step, the concept of creativity, ways to tap into your own creativity, and its links with intuition will all be explored.

ABOUT CREATIVITY

The concept that intuition and creativity are linked makes sense as they are housed in the 'non-dominant' half of the brain, and both are associated with empathy. My personal experience is that when I am spending time being creative in my life, I have more intuitive moments. Personally I am drawn to creative activities, whether tapping into my imagination when reading or writing, or doing craft activities such as beading. The creative side of medicine has always appealed to me, as it is all about finding solutions, and in the past twenty years I have enjoyed the creativity of therapy and guiding individuals or couples towards their goals. Teaching can also be extremely creative as it involves planning content and how to deliver it in a way that actively engages the audience, such as by using stories or humour.

The word 'creativity' comes from the Latin term *creo* meaning 'to create or make'. It refers to the notion of creating something novel and implies that what is created has some kind of use or value. Creativity can therefore refer to making a useful product or item, creating a work of art or finding a novel solution.[33, 34]

A traditional view of creativity was that it was related to Divine inspiration; later, in the eighteenth century, it was linked to the imagination. In recent years creativity has been studied in the fields of psychology, education and technology, and has been viewed as one aspect of human cognition.

Albert Einstein was a creative genius who often spoke about intuition. He referred to intuition and creativity in the following ways, 'There are those who see with their own eyes and feel with their own hearts',[35] and 'To some elementary laws there leads no logical path, but only intuition, supported by being sympathetically in touch with experience.'[36] Abraham Maslow spoke of productive, creative people as having more frequent 'peak experiences', or experiences that transcended their everyday world.[37] Psychosynthesis drew on the ideas of Maslow, acknowledging that we are all creative in our own way; it encouraged the development of creativity in the broadest sense.[38]

Have you ever had the experience of thinking about an issue, sleeping on it, and waking up in the morning with a solution in mind? This is the result of our capacity to have creative insights and is explained by the 'preparation, incubation and insight model' (focusing on the problem, internalising it into the unconscious, finding that a solution emerges), which is useful in problem-solving.[39] It has been found that we can also use our intuition to *boost* our creativity,[40] and to problem-solve. Intuitive people are said to produce more creative solutions.[41]

DEVELOPING YOUR CREATIVITY

In the 1970s I trained in Occupational Therapy (OT). OT developed out of the world wars and the need to offer rehabilitation to the returned soldiers. Originally it involved the use of many and varied activities, such as crafts, workshop-based activities or expressive techniques such as art. The activities were used with therapeutic intent, matching the individual's particular needs. I remember several clients in particular whose lives were turned around by the therapeutic relationship and meaningful activity. When working at a major city hospital, I was asked to see an elderly man from central Australia who had had a heart attack. As I spoke with him, I discovered that he was descended from Afghan camel traders and, as a young boy, he had learnt to create leather whips and saddles for the camels. Now he was elderly and feeling depressed after a heart attack. What would help him to recover?

At the same time I was asked to see two young men in the hospital's burns unit, both of whom had burns to their arms. I chose to get the three men together, and I asked the elderly man to help by teaching the young men some leather work — this activity would assist function to return to their upper limbs. The elderly man obliged over several weeks, and the change in both him and the young men was remarkable. He was doing something of value, while also tapping into his childhood play and creative skills again. The depression lifted and he returned home, often visiting me when he returned to the city. I later said to the two young men that table tennis would be a good activity to further improve their upper limb function. They arrived in the OT department one day to find a large piece of timber and paint. What I hadn't said was that we'd need to build the table first! Humour is an important ingredient in creativity.

One of the main barriers to tapping into our creativity is our conscious mind, which often says, 'I can't draw', 'I don't have time' or 'It has to be perfect.' It was Picasso who said, 'Every child is an artist. The problem is how to remain an artist once we grow up.'[42] Being aware of our self-critical voice is important, and either challenging the thoughts ('I don't have to be an expert or draw perfectly, and I can create some time — this is important') or (from the ACT model of therapy) saying, 'Thank you, brain, for this thought. I am having a thought that ...' and letting it pass through the mind, can help.[43] In my practice, I work from the premise that each of my clients is unique and they are the expert on themselves, with many capabilities to draw upon. If you apply this to creativity, remember that you are unique and have inherent creativity. Complete the following task and tap into your own uniqueness and creativity. Be generous to yourself!

You are unique

In your journal, answer the following questions:
1. What words or images describe your unique self? For example, fun, loyal, friendly, kind ...
2. What is your creative self like? Visual, imaginative, artistic, ingenious, original ...

Other strategies that can assist you to tap into your creativity include:
- Spending quiet time alone or doing quiet activities. Consider doing this routinely.[44]
- Letting go of the need to be right or perfect. Instead, just have fun and go for it![45]
- Going for a walk in nature and experiencing the world in a new creative way. Notice everything that delights you and bring back something from nature; for example, a flower or piece of bark.[46]

- Making a 'creativity' box. Decorate a box however you like and store in it things that arouse your creativity; for example, photos, clippings and pictures from magazines, mementos or quotes.
- Doing one thing at a time (being mindful). If you are being creative, then be in the moment.
- Listening to music.
- Thinking 'I am creative'. According to Choquette, this thought aligns you with your spirit and solutions, rather than problems.[47]
- Doing some strenuous exercise or having a good laugh.[48]
- Try journalling creatively, as suggested by Stephanie Dowrick in her book on creative journal writing. She gives an exercise called 'Observing the Rose', in which you place a rose (or any flower) in front of you (perhaps one you collected on your nature walk!) and write about it. Describe it as someone who has never seen or smelt a rose like it. At the end meditate quietly with your rose, 'not doing, being'.[49]
- Meditating. Given that doing things at a relaxing pace is conducive to creativity (and accessing your subconscious mind),[50] it can be useful to meditate before tapping into your creativity.

Your creative ways

Consider the ways in which you are creative. In your journal, write down how can you tap into your creativity more.

The following list might generate some additional ideas for creative activities. Feel free to add your own!

- Gardening or landscaping
- Reading
- Writing (journal, letters, short stories, poems, books ...)
- Arts and crafts (sewing, felting, drawing, painting, mosaic, card making, scrapbooking)
- Playing with your children or those of friends
- Rearranging furniture, home decorating
- Cooking, cake decorating
- Carpentry
- Tinkering
- Flower arranging
- Doing puzzles
- Telling stories
- Dancing
- Visiting markets and bric-a-brac shops
- Playing a musical instrument or singing
- Meditation and visual imagery
- Walking a labyrinth
- Drawing mandalas
- You might also like to try this meditation focusing on creativity.

CREATIVITY MEDITATION

Make yourself comfortable and let your eyes close. Relax your body and your breath. Now imagine again a path that leads to a cottage and a beautiful garden. Follow the path, feeling the ground under your feet and noticing all that is around you. You look forward to spending time in the garden, but you go inside the cottage for a little while first. There is a room for creating in the cottage, with a large table and shelves full of paper, pens, glue, boxes, paints and many craft materials. You are curious about the room and explore the shelves. What creative project comes to mind? Spend some time creating at the table, using whatever materials you like.

Once finished in the cottage, you see a basket for you to take outside. You head out into the garden with your basket. Explore the garden and see what you can find — perhaps there are interesting leaves or bark, maybe feathers or colourful flowers. Enjoy collecting what you would like. Then, when you are ready, head back into the creative room. Here you can spend some time looking at what you have found, noticing the colours and textures of these items. Nature is very creative. Then contemplate what you would like to do with them. You might decide to put them in a box and keep them. You could decorate that box. You might decide to make a collage by sticking them on a piece of paper or you might want to draw one of them. Just enjoy being creative for a while.

When you are ready, you can leave the cottage and its garden and come back to the here and now.

___

MANDALAS

Mandalas were mentioned in the list of creative activities above. I became curious about them five years ago when I came across a woman selling mandalas at a market. She spoke of mandalas being a meditative art form used to tap into the unconscious. She had pre-drawn mandalas to sell but she would also sit with an individual and, working intuitively, draw a mandala that related particularly to them at that moment in time. I had a mandala drawn and it fitted with where I perceived myself to be at that time. She suggested keeping it close — for example, on my desk at work — to enable me to see it, reflect on it and work through related emotions.

Mandalas shift focus from the outer world to the inner world. They provide a symbolic view of the inner emotions, needs, pain and inspiration, and are thought to reflect the unconscious mind or Higher Self. Hence they assist with insight and intuition. 'Mandala' itself is a Sanskrit word meaning 'sacred circle',[51] and mandalas begin with a circular form which is then filled in spontaneously. Jung, who introduced the mandala to Western thought, had significant personal experiences when drawing mandalas and found people were drawn to them in their dreams.[52] Mandala art has been used throughout the world in spiritual transformation practices and in Tibetan Buddhism for thousands of years. Navajo sand painters use circular forms to frame their drawings and in healing rites, and mandala art is said to activate the healing powers of the mind.[53]

Mandalas are also used for meditation. The book *Healing Mandalas* by Lisa Tenzin-Dolma features intricate mandalas, each involving symbols and representing different things; for example, there is a lotus meditation, representing showing one's inner beauty to the outside world.[54] You can meditate on the mandalas by taking a few slow breaths, then settling into normal steady breathing while resting your gaze on the mandala, keeping your eyes softly focused, and allowing the image to soak into your consciousness. At some point there will be a feeling of connectedness with the mandala. When you're ready to stop, take another few deep slow breaths and then breathe normally, close your eyes for a moment, and then stretch. Enjoy the feeling of peace. Consider any insights or intuitive ideas and write them down.[55]

About two years ago, I attended an art therapy class that

included completing a series of mandalas related to the chakra system. 'Chakras', from the Sanskrit word for 'wheel', are described in Hindu and Buddhist yogic literature and are thought to form an interconnected energy system throughout the body. The flow of energy within this system is said to be related to physical, emotional and spiritual wellbeing.[56] Seven main chakras are described, each aligned with an endocrine gland and a nerve plexus.[57, 58] The chakras are referred to as the root, sacral, solar plexus, heart, throat, third eye and crown chakras.[59] The chakras and their functions are summarised in the following table, adapted from the work of psychiatrist and intuitive Judith Orloff.[60]

CHAKRA	LOCATION	FUNCTION	COLOUR
First (the root)	Genital area	Sexuality	Red
Second (sacral)	5cm below the belly button, midline	Sexuality, nurturing, balance	Orange
Third	Solar plexus	Emotions, power, control	Yellow
Fourth (heart chakra)	5cm above the diaphragm, midline	Compassion, love	Green
Fifth	Throat	Communication, speaking your truth	Cobalt Blue
Sixth (third eye)	Forehead, between eyebrows	Intuition, intellect	Indigo Blue
Seventh (crown chakra)	Top of head	Spirituality	Purple

Life domains mandala

This creative and reflective exercise is based on the different areas or domains in your life, such as family and friends, education and personal development, leisure and creativity. In your journal, draw a circle (a mandala) — this will be become a 'map' of your life. Now imagine a typical week or month and consider the activities that you do and the roles you play. Be aware of how much time and effort you give to each one. Now, make a 'map' of this by dividing up the circle into sections to represent the different domains. Consider where creativity and intuition fit on your map. You can use words, colours, images or symbols to represent each domain.

Take some time to consider where creativity is evident in your circle and where it sits. How much space have you given it? Are you happy with the time you spend on this domain, or do you want to change this?

To complete this section on creativity, reflect on the words of Stephanie Dowrick:

Creativity can be a way of living that is open, spirited, engaged ... and uplifting.[61]

ENHANCE YOUR CREATIVITY

- Creativity enhances your intuition, and intuition enhances your creativity.
- They are both housed in the 'non-dominant' brain and are linked with empathy.
- Creativity can refer to making a useful product, creating a work of art or finding a novel solution.
- When you create something it doesn't have to be perfect.
- You have uniqueness and creativity.
- To develop your creativity, enjoy quiet time, go for a walk in nature, make a 'creativity' box, listen to music, do some exercise, have a good laugh or write in your journal.
- Mandalas are a meditative art form that are thought to reflect the unconscious mind and assist with intuition.

STEP 5: ACCESS YOUR UNCONSCIOUS MIND

The section on mandalas, which are said to *reflect* the unconscious mind, segues into discussion about *accessing* the unconscious mind. There is agreement in the neuroscience literature that intuition is related to the unconscious. You will remember that Jung described intuition as unconscious perception and how intuition taps into implicit processes and knowledge in the body and brain. We also know that intuition predominantly sits in the non-dominant hemisphere of the brain and is often derived from images, feelings, physical sensations and metaphors. In this step we will explore the nature and role of the unconscious mind and consider some ways in which we can access our unconscious to aid us in developing our intuition, including signs and symbols and dreams.

THE UNCONSCIOUS AND THE HIGHER SELF

In psychotherapy, the conscious and unconscious minds are often referred to. When explaining hypnotherapy to a client, for example, I often talk about the conscious and unconscious minds in terms of an iceberg. The conscious mind is that part of the iceberg above the water; it involves our conscious awareness of what is around us and our conscious decisions. The unconscious mind, on the other hand, is like the greater mass of ice below the water. It houses our memories of past experiences, a great deal of knowledge and contains a range of unconscious beliefs that we build up during our lifetime about ourselves and the world. It also wants what is best for us and can guide us.

You will remember from Chapter 1 that psychosynthesis

identifies the personal or conscious self ('I'); an unconscious; and, in addition, a spiritual source ('Self'). It takes the view that we often get caught up with our emotions, thoughts and sensations, and this limits our ability to be guided by 'Self.' Another name for Self is 'Higher Self' or 'wise inner self'. I tend to use the term 'inner wisdom'. Interestingly, modern-day therapies such as hypnotherapy, ACT and Dialectical Behaviour Therapy (DBT) refer to an 'observing self' or 'wise mind'.[62, 63] This refers to the part of the mind that notices our thoughts and feelings, but is calm and non-judgmental.[64] DBT refers to the wise mind as being akin to intuition and also refers to accessing a 'Higher Power', such as God or the universe.[65]

Current authors such as Penney Peirce refer to the conscious mind, the unconscious mind, and the 'Higher Self'. She has the view that when intuition is sourced from the unconscious, it often comes through the five senses or in the physical body. The Higher Self is described as understanding the interconnection of everything that exists in time and space, so it can generate global perceptions and transcendent experiences. It is that part of you that contains higher purpose.[66] When intuition is sourced from your Higher Self, it might be like a light is turning on in your head, involving a blending of all your senses and an all-over 'direct knowing' often accompanied by a feeling of openheartedness.

Activities that we have highlighted that can help you tap into your unconscious mind and intuition include being self-aware, practising meditation and mindfulness, enjoying imaginative and creative activities (such as music, drawing and mandalas) and relating to others with awareness and empathy. Writing is a great way to access your inner wisdom. Do you have a problem that you want to reflect on and seek guidance with? Stephanie Dowrick suggests writing a letter about it in detail and then finishing with one of these questions: 'The insight I most value is ... ?', 'The action I need to take is ... ?' or 'I am most grateful to see that ... ?'[67]

A number of psychotherapeutic approaches incorporate work with the unconscious mind, including NLP and hypnosis. Some of the techniques used are ideomotor finger signals and pendulums. With ideomotor finger signals, the therapist explains to the person in the trance state that communication with the unconscious mind can be set up through finger signals, and that the individual does not need to make any conscious effort to move the fingers. The index finger is allocated to indicate 'yes', the thumb 'no', and the little finger 'not sure' or 'don't know'. Sometimes the person will feel the movements like a twitch or feeling of electricity. Questions can then be asked and responses are given.

Pendulums are often mentioned in texts on intuition. I was interested to see them used during NLP training. A pendulum has a weighted part (often a crystal or stone) attached to a chain or cord. The individual sets up 'yes' or 'no' responses with their pendulum and, again, questions can be asked. I have found the ideomotor signals very useful in practice, but I feel less sure about the pendulum. Experience will tell!

SYMBOLS AND SIGNS

Truth did not come into the world naked,
but it came in types and images.

THE GOSPEL OF PHILIP

Sometimes our intuition emerges through signs or symbols, sometimes in our awake state and sometimes in dreams. This is certainly my experience in life. Have you had the experience of interpreting an occurrence in life as a sign or have symbols brought meaning to you? In the movie *Under the Tuscan Sun*, the elderly woman selling her house in Italy needed a sign to go ahead with the sale. This came in the form of bird droppings landing on the protagonist, 'a lucky sign'. Symbols have occurred in all cultures and they express human nature, gathering meaning over hundreds or thousands of years. They have been used in ritual and prayer, art, psychology and marketing.[68] According to Peirce, symbols convey a large amount of 'encoded' information in a powerful and meaningful way. Symbols can lead us. Consider, for example, a country's national flag. And many corporations represent their identity with logos (or symbols). The table overleaf highlights some common symbols and their meaning.[69]

Peirce provides a meditation to assist with your intuition, based on symbols.[70] I have adapted it on page 109. She suggests that you develop a personal relationship with your symbol, by looking out for it around you, or perhaps collecting images of it in your journal. I have adopted the symbol of an owl for myself, as there is so much to learn every day, so much wisdom to acquire and share.

EXAMPLES OF SYMBOLS	MEANING
Lotus plant, which grows in mud at the bottom of the pond, with the flower raising itself above the water to reveal its beauty.	Growth and enlightenment
Dragon	In the East the dragon is a symbol of joy, dynamism and good health
The butterfly	The powers of transformation and immortality
The lion	Royalty, protection and wisdom
The tree of life	Harmony, rewards of spiritual growth (fruits)
The fig tree	Enlightenment
The rose	Light, love and life
Jade	Perfection, immortality and magical powers
Sapphire	Blue of the heavens, truth and contemplation

PERSONAL SYMBOL MEDITATION

Make yourself comfortable and close your eyes. Breathe and allow yourself to relax physically and mentally. Then ask your body and mind to bring you a personal symbol to assist you with your intuition development. Notice what image speaks to you. Let it come into your mind. If no image comes into your mind, that's fine too. Perhaps you will become aware of it in coming days. Enjoy the relaxation. Then, when you are ready, open your eyes in the here and now.

Signs are more subtle than symbols and rely on the individual finding meaning in them. I heard Madonna interviewed about a movie that she directed on the lives of Wallis Simpson and Edward VIII. She said that she was initially torn about whether or not to pursue the project, but a series of signs helped her to decide. In one instance, she heard the doorbell ring and answered the door to find no one there. However, a furniture removal truck was parked directly opposite her house, and the company's name was the same as Wallis's mother's maiden name. She interpreted this as a sign to go ahead with the project.

Gia, a counsellor whom I interviewed for this book, asks herself questions in the morning and looks for signs during the day to assist with answers. Signs might come from 'number plates on the road, books that catch [her] attention in the shops or online, billboards, movies, sounds, animals that cross [her] path'. I too have had some interesting experiences with signs. One night I was driving home to my house in the hills. I was going through a particularly challenging time and I spoke out loud to my father (who had died some years previously), asking him for a sign that things were going to improve. The next moment a white owl flew across the road in front of me — I saw him in the moonlight and the car lights. There was the sign! Owls symbolise wisdom. My father had plenty of that and he loved all animals, including white birds. I got the message that things would get better.

I am not going to leave out my mother, as I have a story about socks! In her later years my mother had poor circulation and liked to always have socks on her feet to keep them warm. It is interesting that psychics giving readings will pick up on this sort of thing. I had a reading a few years ago and the psychic mentioned my deceased father keeping my mother's feet and hands warm while she was in the nursing home. Just before Christmas, I came into my house after work, saw Mum's picture and said out loud, 'This is the first Christmas without you and I will miss you.' Shortly afterwards I was putting the laundry away and I came across one of my mother's labelled socks from the nursing home! I don't quite know how it got there. The next day, I took suitcases in to work as we were moving practice locations. One of the girls was packing things into the suitcase when she came across an item. She brought it in to me and said, 'What are these doing in the suitcase?' She was holding a pair of socks with my mother's name on them. I just laughed!

DREAMS

Who looks outside, dreams; who looks inside, awakes.
JUNG

Everybody is familiar with dreams, pleasant ones as well as

nightmares. There are numerous cases in history where people have credited dreams with helping them to compose music or finish an invention. Have you ever had dreams that have given you insights or helped you find an answer to a problem? Or have you had dreams that perhaps involved premonitions? Dreams are vital to humans. Babies spend a lot of time dreaming, suggesting it is an important state for brain development.[71] Dreams seem to involve the mind (conscious and unconscious) processing experiences, memories and feelings. They might provide constructive messages for us; for example, offering insight into how to deal with an issue. Have you ever been thinking about an issue, gone to sleep and had a dream, and awakened with more clarity the next day? Dreams can assist us to process how we really feel about things.

Jung was fascinated by dreams and saw them as a means to bring our psyche into balance.[72] He explored their meaning, suggesting that some individuals are able to access the 'collective unconscious' through dreams, and he talked about 'archetypes' appearing in dreams.[73] These he defined as innate behavioural patterns or ways of responding to human experiences such as death or relationships. Examples are 'the Miraculous Child', a symbol of new possibility or growth, or 'the Great Mother', a symbol of rebirth and service to others.[74] In relation to dream symbols, it is generally thought that they can have multiple meanings. Most symbols seem to have a personal meaning, depending on our life experience. A house, for example, might symbolise a place of shelter and safety, but this will depend on your experience with houses in general or even a particular house. Jung saw that dreams had to be worked through with the individual to determine their meaning,[75] and this is the approach that I take if clients ask about their dreams.

When I was in my early twenties, I visited the United Kingdom to work in a psychiatric hospital for several months and to travel. While I was there I went to a workshop on dreams. We were asked to take a recent dream and recall it in detail. This involved talking through the dream several times. It was fascinating how much detail came to mind through repeated recollections. Once the detail was there, we focused on the emotions involved in the dream. I had dreamt about going down a flight of stairs and into a room. This led to another room in which an elderly person was sitting with a rug over their knees. The person felt alone. As we worked through the dreams, we learnt that each aspect of the dream was about ourselves; I certainly felt alone at times in the UK, going to work and then home to a bedsit, not really knowing anyone nearby.

Can dreams tell us about our futures? Many authors seem to think so. Jung apparently worked with a businessman who became involved in mountain climbing. The man dreamt about stepping off a mountain into the air. Jung is reported to have warned him about the nature of his dream, but the man ignored him and later died mountain climbing.[76] I have had some interesting dreams over the years but those that stand out are related to premonitions. These dreams were particularly vivid and seemed so real that I was always shaken by them. The first one I really paid attention to was when I was about seventeen years of age. I dated a young man for several years and was close to his family, in particular his younger sister. One night I dreamt that I was holding a baby and the baby died in my arms. I remember thinking that I didn't usually dream of death or babies. The next day I had lunch with his mother and older sister and I said that I had had this vivid dream and feared someone was going to die. I was unaware that the younger sister had been diagnosed with cancer. She died three months later.

Being more aware of your dreams and interpreting them is seen as an important part of developing intuition. To raise awareness, it is best to record your dreams as soon as you wake up.[77] When I undertook the dream workshop, the facilitator suggested keeping a journal and a pen by the bed. On awakening, you lie quiet and still, focusing on recalling the dream(s). Then you write down in detail what you recall. You will find that by doing this regularly, you will recall more about your dreams. Orloff suggests that you pay attention to and record images or symbols in your dreams to which you are especially drawn or that move you. The next step is to meditate quietly and hold the symbol in your mind, asking to be shown its significance. Then pay attention to any intuitive images, scenarios, memories or physical sensations that arise, as they will assist in understanding the symbol. She also suggests writing a question in your journal before you go to sleep and then reflecting on the answer via your dreams the next day.[78]

ACCESS YOUR UNCONSCIOUS MIND

- Intuition taps into knowledge in the body and brain, and is often derived from images, feelings, physical sensations and metaphors.
- The unconscious mind can guide us.
- The 'Higher Self', or inner wisdom, is described as capable of generating transcendent experience related to your purpose.
- Activities that assist include meditation, creative activity, awareness and empathy; some therapeutic techniques also work with the unconscious.
- Intuition may come through symbols and signs.
- Dreams can provide us with useful information and we can develop our understanding of dreams by journalling them.

STEP 6: TAP INTO POSITIVITY

This section focuses on developing your positivity and includes strategies such as being kind and compassionate, practising gratitude and finding your purpose. These practices are important as they assist us to feel positive emotions and open us up to think expansively. There is a model in positive psychology called the 'broaden-and-build' theory that relates to this concept: 'Positive emotions open our hearts and our minds, making us more receptive and more creative.'[79] My hypothesis is that they also open us up to possibilities and intuitive experiences.

BE KIND AND COMPASSIONATE

No act of kindness, no matter how small, is ever wasted.

AESOP

Earlier this year I was fortunate enough to go out to lunch with my son and five of his friends. I say 'fortunate' as they are all nineteen or twenty and I think it was rather nice of them to want to sit around a table with a mum and chat! There was a lot of light-hearted discussion about the New Year's Eve celebrations the night before down at the beach near where we were staying. My son then mentioned a preacher who had been at the beach shouting about 'sin' and 'fearing God'. The young men then asked, 'What do you think, Cate? Is it all about fear?' I responded, 'I don't believe it is. Actually to me, it's all about love.' Several of them agreed with me and then the conversation went back to the waves!

Ever since I was young, I've wanted to write books. In fact, during each school holiday, I would pick a topic and produce a mini-book. Part of me knew my purpose even then! One time I wrote a series of little booklets on love. My older sister Susan was very much a role model for me, so I wrote them as a gift for her. One was about love being like a flower — the flower starts as a small bud and over time gradually blossoms into a beautiful flower! I cannot really remember the other ones, but I still come back to the flower in my mind quite often. When I was referring to love in my conversation with the young men over lunch, it was love in the broadest sense — for individuals and among humankind; and if you have faith in God or a Higher Power, love is a central part of this faith.

This section is about giving love, by being kind and compassionate, to both others and yourself. There is growing evidence that practising loving-kindness creates more positivity. Researcher Barbara Frederickson describes how loving-kindness meditation evolved from ancient Buddhist mind-training practices. In this meditation you train your emotion towards warm and compassionate feelings in an open-hearted way. You direct these feelings to yourself and then to an ever-widening circle of others.[80] I suggest that loving-kindness practices also help us to create a state of mind more in tune with our intuition. Spiritual writers such as William Bloom agree.[81]

When you think of kind and compassionate people, who comes to mind? Perhaps someone you know or have worked with? Or maybe Mother Teresa or the Dalai Lama? The Buddha said we should 'have compassion for all beings, rich and poor alike; each has their suffering'. Compassion is empathy for the suffering of others, so to have compassion for others you must first notice their suffering and then feel warmth or caring and a desire to help in some way. Compassion means that you offer understanding and kindness to others when they make mistakes or fail, rather than judging them harshly.[82] Deepak Chopra, a physician and teacher, speaks of the importance of letting go of judgments and labelling. Then we are more able to be intuitive and our heart grows.[83] Hence, acceptance and being non-judgmental are important aspects of compassion and lead to being able to give unconditional love.

Kindness can assist others and lift your own spirits. In fact, kindness not only gives us pleasure but it has been shown to improve our wellbeing. For example, a study at Harvard University in the United States involved showing students a film about Mother Teresa and then checking their immunoglobulin levels (integral in the immune response). They were found to be elevated. Another study at Harvard found those students who volunteered their time or money were 42 per cent more likely to describe themselves as happy. And across the Atlantic at the University of Cambridge, researchers found that when students saw someone helping another person, it caused them to want to go out and do something for someone else.[84] Kindness is not only good for us, it's catching!

To experience the benefits for yourself, try the following adaptation of 'The Inner Smile' meditation.[85]

'THE INNER SMILE' MEDITATION

Make yourself comfortable and let your eyes close. Breathe into the abdomen and let it rise and fall softly. Focus on the heart area and feel it open as you reflect on an attitude of kindness and generosity. When have you received kindness and generosity? When have you given kindness and generosity? Feel your 'inner smile' grow.

Now focus on your body and give it the same care as

you would a child or an injured animal. You have a kind and loving attitude to your own body and you see your body as a chalice, allowing your inner smile to fill it with love. Enjoy the kind and loving feelings.

When you are ready, open your eyes and come back to the room.

One of the traps in life is comparison with others. We are hardwired to compare as part of our tools for survival. If we come across an individual who looks threatening, then comparison is important. Our mind assesses whether they are dangerous and whether we should flee. But comparisons can also work against us and harm us. I quite often see young women or men in my practice and a common issue they experience is comparing themselves to others and thinking they don't measure up. Other people are always 'smarter' or 'thinner' or 'more popular'. The result is that these young people are often left feeling sad or anxious, withdrawing from others, thinking harshly about themselves and perhaps self-harming.

Practising acts of kindness towards yourself and others can help to bring more peace and joy to your life. Self-compassion means you are able to be kind and understanding towards yourself when faced with your personal failings, instead of criticising and judging yourself harshly.[86] As discussed, kindness begets kindness and the power of kindness cannot be underestimated. Engaging in random acts of kindness can often lead to you feeling more connected with others and more empathic, as well as more positive within yourself. Some of the unexpected outcomes of acting with kindness can be an increased sense of peace, love and trust.[87]

To remind yourself of the value of loving-kindness during the day, recite this ancient Tibbetan Buddhist poem on loving-kindness to yourself.

The Loving-kindness poem

May I be filled with loving-kindness
May I be well
May I be peaceful and at ease
May I be happy

Or you can meditate on loving-kindness regularly. Below is a meditation that I have adapted from Barbara Frederickson.[88]

LOVING-KINDNESS MEDITATION

Make yourself comfortable and let your eyes close. Focus your attention on the breath and relax. Focus too on the region of your heart. Once grounded in the feeling of your own heart, reflect on a person for whom you feel warm, tender and compassionate feelings. This could be a child, partner or even a pet. Visualise or imagine yourself being with this loved one and notice how you feel. Extend loving-kindness to them by saying, 'May you be well, may you be at ease, may you be happy and at peace.'

Hold onto the warm and compassionate feelings. And now extend the warm feeling to yourself. Cherish yourself as you do others. Allow your heart to radiate with love. When you are ready, radiate your warm and compassionate feelings to others, first to a person you know well, then gradually call to mind others with whom you have connections. Ultimately you can extend loving-kindness to all if you choose.

When you are ready come back to the room, opening your eyes. Notice and hold onto your positive feelings.

Affirmations were originally made popular by counsellor and author Louise Hay. I recently heard her speak at a conference where I was reminded of their value. Affirmations are statements said in the present tense, involving positive sentiment. An example might be, 'I am feeling calmer and more confident each day.' The positive words remove self-criticism, lift our spirits and encourage self-compassion and belief. Louise Hay explored the relationship between mind and body in her writing. At the conference, Hay invited the audience to use affirmations and to speak them into a mirror. Quite a challenge at times! To finish this section on self-compassion, and in keeping with our garden metaphor, here is a powerful meditation that will help you to recognise your strengths and experience compassion for yourself. It is based on a hypnosis script that I came across some years ago.[89]

TREE MEDITATION

Make yourself comfortable and let your eyes close. Relax the body and mind. Breathe and relax. Imagine a beautiful garden. Within the garden is a beautiful tree. Approach the tree and see its strong roots, its broad trunk and leafy branches spreading upward. It has firm roots into the ground and marks on its trunk. It has grown steadily and survived wind and storms. It is truly amazing. It not only draws what it needs from the earth and sky each day (water, sunlight and carbon dioxide), but it gives so much back (shelter, oxygen, food). The tree grows stronger each day and it thrives on care and compassion from us.

You might not think it initially, but when you contemplate you are a lot like the tree. You have strengths like the tree, you give and take, and you have weathered storms. But you are even more amazing than the tree, as you can speak, move, think and love as well. Look inside yourself and see your strengths and abilities. And like the tree, you thrive on care and compassion. Now go closer to the tree and give the tree a hug. Feel its energy. Feel your own energy and allow yourself to recognise your strengths and to feel compassion for yourself.

When you are ready, gradually come back to the here and now and open your eyes.

PRACTISE GRATITUDE

When you arise in the morning think of what
a precious privilege it is to be alive — to breathe,
to think, to enjoy, to love.
MARCUS AURELIUS

Gratitude means different things to different people. For some of us it means thanking someone. For others it evokes an appreciation of life and 'counting our blessings'. It is good to think about and practise gratitude as it has been found to be an antidote to negative emotions such as envy and worry. People who experience gratitude have been shown to be happier, more energetic and more hopeful.[90] I came across an article in a newspaper about a woman called Marie-Therese who lived with 'locked-in syndrome' for seventeen years. Despite only being able to move her eyelids, she expressed '100 reasons why life is great'. This became her epitaph. Her reasons included the following: 'Every time I see my beautiful sons, especially when all three of them visit together and we are a family; being able to communicate [by blinking]; being taken out in my wheelchair for a concert, and witnessing the best side of human nature every day in the form of the kind nurses who tend to me.'[91] I found her list very moving and a reminder to treasure all that we have.

Sonja Lyubomirsky, a psychologist working in the field of positive psychology, explains the many benefits of practising gratitude:

1. It allows us to embrace positive life experiences and to take satisfaction from them.

2. Expressing gratitude reinforces our sense of self-worth. Appreciating how much others do for us and how much we achieve ourselves gives us greater confidence.

3. It takes the focus away from the negative aspects of our life and places it on what we value.

4. Gratitude helps people to cope with stress and trauma. Appreciating life may be used as a coping method to help reinterpret negative life events and the lessons we learn from them or the strengths we develop.

5. Expressing gratitude promotes moral behaviour. Grateful people are more likely to help others and be less likely to be overly materialistic.

6. Gratitude can help to build and strengthen relationships. Studies have shown that those who feel gratitude towards others experience closer and higher quality relationships with those individuals.

7. Expressing gratitude can help diminish comparisons with others. Being grateful for the wonderful things you have (either personal characteristics or material) distracts from envy of what others have.

8. Gratitude is incompatible with what are commonly perceived as 'negative' emotions (such as sadness and anger) and may deter unhelpful feelings (such as bitterness or greed).

9. It prevents us from falling susceptible to 'hedonic adaptation' (looking for more to make us happy, adapting to more, then wanting more again).[92]

To assist you in tuning into more positivity and, I would suggest, intuition in your life, focus on practising gratitude more often in what you think and say. Consider keeping a gratitude journal and noting down things you have felt grateful for — nothing is too small or insignificant to write in your journal. You might be grateful for a friend's support, a good sleep or the sunshine. In research Lyubomirsky carried out on the effect of gratitude journals, she found that they were helpful to our mood and that the optimum frequency for writing in the journal was not once a day or once a month, but once a week.[93] So get started now!

> ## What are you grateful for?
>
> In your journal write down six things that you are grateful for today!

FIND YOUR PURPOSE

The purpose of life is a life of purpose.
ROBERT BYRNE

Judith Orloff is both highly intuitive and a psychiatrist. She describes her purpose as being to heal and share with the world information about intuition.[94] She says that if we follow our intuition, we will find our purpose. We all have gifts and our purpose is related to these. Her own experience was that she was an intuitive child with parents who were doctors and unable to make sense of her dreams and premonitions. After Orloff had the experience of her grandfather visiting her in a dream the night that he died, her parents told her not to talk about her dreams any more. As a result, she suppressed her feelings and experiences and later got into drugs. At one point she was sent to a psychiatrist, who was fortunately kind and understanding and referred her to people who were open to her experiences. She became involved in research in the field of parapsychology and around this time had a dream. In it, she was told to study medicine and share her knowledge about intuition.[95] That is what she has done.

I think my purpose is to help people, whether through medicine or writing. I started school very young and finished young, so I wasn't sure what to do when I left. I was stronger in the Arts at the time and so didn't even contemplate Medicine. Instead, I studied Occupational Therapy (OT), which gave me a good grounding in health. I loved the intellectual challenge of Anatomy and Physiology and so decided to apply for Medicine a year or so after finishing OT. Serendipitously, at the time there was a medical course in my hometown that did not require a science background but admitted a number of mature-age students based on their high-school scores, their tertiary performance and a written piece. I found myself fortunate enough to be studying Medicine.

I remember finding some of the subjects in first year difficult and I studied very long hours. One subject, Physical Chemistry, was interesting but particularly challenging for me because of the equations and mathematics involved. In the final year exam, I worked through the paper as best I could. With quite a few questions I was able to work out part of the solution but not the final answer. I remember praying that my efforts would be enough to pass. But as I checked through my paper one last time, I suddenly found that answers literally came into my mind. At the time, I couldn't believe it — and neither could the lecturer! I can't explain this experience other than to say that the answers simply appeared intuitively. My exam results enabled me to progress to the next year, on track with my purpose.

Finding your purpose

Consider your own story now and, in your journal, reflect on these questions related to the past year.

1. When you look back on the past twelve months, what do you feel most positive about or proud of?
2. What did you enjoy the most?
3. What is the most important thing for you to learn from the past year?
4. Do you think this learning is related to your purpose?
5. What do you see as your purpose in life?

It took me a while to find my purpose in life. I completed several degrees and worked in many settings. I now feel that I am aligned with my purpose. My son Alex finished school a year or so ago. He thought about various careers and at the end of his final year of school decided to apply to Physiotherapy. However, he wanted a gap year to work and travel and also undertake some related courses. By the end of that year, he was not so sure about Physio and instead enrolled in a Bachelor of Education. But after a while, teaching didn't feel like the right path for him either. Alex has now decided to pursue his main passion, music. He describes his purpose as being 'to play music to everyone in the world, to express my emotions through the music and allow the audience to do the same'. His decision feels right because it is aligned with his passion and purpose.

I asked several of the people I interviewed about their purpose. This is what they said.

Lynn said her purpose is to be of service to others in her role as an active listener, to 'give time and space for others to be heard, acknowledged and nurtured'. This gives Lynn joy and happiness. She sees 'following your bliss' as purpose and supporting expressions of creativity from within.

Melanie said that her 'passion is to express myself creatively, and my purpose is to share this with the world'. Through her work she aims to inspire and uplift every person she comes into contact with.

Heather described her purpose as helping her clients find peace, particularly young women. She is passionate about her work, and helping her clients to 'shine'.

So what is purpose all about? Purpose is defined as the reason for which something is done or exists. Let's bring passion into the equation. Passion is defined as great enthusiasm.[96] If we combine these two definitions, then purpose is about doing what you love and perhaps were meant to do.[97] I have a picture at home that says 'Live what you love' — a great reminder for me each day.

A good starting point for exploring your purpose is to look at your values as we did in Chapter 4. Do you have role models or individuals who seem to live a life consistent with their values? Nelson Mandela was prepared to go to prison for his values. Mother Teresa lived a life as a nun in India for her values (including faith and service to the poor and dying).

Your role models

In your journal, answer the following questions:
1. Who are your role models?
2. What values of theirs do you admire?
3. How have they influenced your life and actions?

Consider too whether you are living a fulfilling life with purpose. If the answer is 'yes', that's wonderful. If you answer 'no', or 'not sure', then it's important to understand the influence of your thoughts and beliefs on your sense of purpose. So many times I have heard clients say, 'I couldn't do that.' But we don't often hear young children saying it. It seems that as we grow up we take on board a range of limiting ideas, such as 'I'm not smart enough' or 'I'm not good enough'. Consider whether any of your thoughts are holding you back from fulfilling your purpose.

A useful technique for raising awareness of our thoughts about self comes from a book by social worker Carolynn Hillman called *Recovery of Your Self-Esteem*. It ties in with one of the most useful therapies, namely Cognitive Behaviour Therapy (CBT), which is based on the view that thoughts and beliefs affect our feelings and behaviour, and are in turn affected by them. This technique involves three steps:

Recognise your positive points and strengths by making a list of 'What I like about myself: my positive points'. Reflect on this list and add to it over time; maybe ask others for ideas. Read the list regularly and acknowledge your positive points.

Recognise the 'inner critic' or the inner negative voice and make a list of 'Things I do not like about myself: negative points'. Consider whose voice is being critical — has the criticism been internalised from other people?

Then reassess these negative things and be fairer on yourself. Are the statements too critical? Can they be re-worded so they are less harsh? Try reframing them — an example would be 'I tend to be quiet in front of others, but I am working on talking with people more'.[98]

Remember that our positive and negative traits can be like two sides of a coin. A strength, such as being determined, can also be viewed as a negative quality at times — determination might be interpreted as stubbornness. Sometimes we only view the negative aspect. A parent might complain that their child is opinionated and feisty. They might view this negatively, forgetting that the positive view is that their child is able to stand up for themselves — very useful given that peer-pressure can be such a powerful force in adolescence.

From negative to positive

In your journal, work through the three steps outlined in the technique above. Remember to treat yourself with self-compassion!
1. What I like about myself: my positive points.
2. Things I do not like about myself: my negative points (e.g. I can't cook).
3. Rewrite the negatives (e.g. I can cook a number of recipes but I would like to expand my repertoire).

Sometimes part of us might seem to want to change our self-belief or direction in life, but another part might seem to hold us back. We could journal a conversation between these two parts or we could use a powerful NLP technique for integrating what's seen as two 'parts' of our mind. In this technique, the two conflicting parts of the mind are identified; for example, the part of the mind that feels worthwhile and the part that feels undeserving. The therapist then asks the person to hold their hands out in front of them and imagine each part on a different hand. The client then describes the part, what it looks like and what it feels like. Individuals often see an image or shape or experience a sensation of lightness or heaviness. They are then asked about the purpose of each of these parts until the highest purpose is identified. Often this is the same for each part and is about peace or happiness.[99]

We might need to work on enhancing our sense of self-belief. Remember to celebrate your successes and achievements! You might wish to be informed by your broader belief system (whether that be related to God, the universe, Buddhism or a Higher Power) when considering purpose. I have always wanted to be of service to people and part of this, I am sure, came from having a family who valued service, a Christian upbringing and, later, broader spiritual influences. I like the idea from Orloff that we all have gifts and our intuition guides us to use these gifts.[100] Adrienne also has words of wisdom, suggesting doing what you love and were meant to do'.[101] She advises that sometimes you just need to have faith that things will work out, that sometimes we need to take a leap of faith, trusting that we know ourselves and will end up where we need to go. She suggests that we keep our focus on that which gives us energy, for which we have passion, and to move with trust in that direction.

TAP INTO POSITIVITY

- Positive emotions make us more receptive and more creative, opening us up to possibilities and intuitive experiences.
- Practise loving-kindness towards yourself and others.
- Compassion involves letting go of judgments; when we do this we are more able to be intuitive and our heart grows.
- Practising acts of kindness can help bring more

peace and joy to our life.
- Practising gratitude assists us to be more positive and hopeful. Keep a gratitude journal.
- If we follow our intuition and passion, we will find our purpose.
- Purpose is about doing what we love and were meant to do.
- Be less self-critical and recognise your strengths.
- Celebrate your successes; trust in your abilities.

STEP 7: APPLY INTUITION IN YOUR EVERYDAY AND WORKING LIFE

I am a very practical person in many ways and for me knowledge needs to be translated into action. In the same way, intuition needs to be practical. Hence the very practical steps in this book. If you think about our garden metaphor, a garden epitomises the practical. Creating the garden involves practical work; the completed garden produces flowers with pollen, trees that provide shelter and oxygen, and we can also have fruit trees and a vegetable patch to provide food. So in this step we will consider how can we bring intuition into our lives in very practical ways.

If you think back to the first two chapters, a number of important messages emerged from the review of intuition through different lenses, such as intuition and reasoning being complementary, and intuition being like a compass in life. These ideas are important in relation to applying intuition in your everyday life. Personally, I value my rational thinking and

I listen to my intuition. I have learnt to nurture my intuition and to trust my clinical intuition. For my intuition to be active, I need space for it in my life; I need time for rest, time for beauty, and I need to engage in creative pursuits. I practise mindfulness and meditation some of the time, I am not always in tune with my body, I am curious about my dreams and I endeavour to practise compassion and gratitude. Let's now consider how you can translate ideas such as these into practical measures for incorporating intuition into your everyday life.

LISTEN TO YOUR BODY

One practical measure we can put into practice each day is to tune into our body. We have talked about the body and how it sends signals to us in Chapter 3. In this day and age, we are often more aware of what is going on in our heads or outside ourselves than in our own body. We might work in offices or at home, spend a lot of time on computers or watching television and not much time doing physical activities. Listening to your body is a positive way to apply intuition in life and stay true to yourself. I tune into my gut-feelings when I meet new people. I find that I get an impression quite quickly about them. At times I have doubted this feeling, worrying that it is judgmental or inaccurate, but I have learnt to listen to it as most times it's proven to be right. This is a very useful life skill that can help us to avoid many problems in relating to others.

Orloff talks about noticing what the body is sensing and the corresponding signals it sends us.[102] Our body will tell us if we are comfortable with a particular place, person or choice in life. Have you had the experience of just knowing that a new job, house or relationship was right or not right? Recently, I was watching a

British television show about people looking for a house in the country for a sea change. A young couple were looking at old farmhouses and when they went into the last house the husband expressed that he did not feel comfortable with the layout. He couldn't put his finger on it but it just didn't feel right to him. His wife liked the house but respected his reaction to it so the house was off the list for them.

We can have the experience of 'knowing without knowing how we know' about a person, place, job or decision. Many clients have shared with me their gut-feelings about these things. Sometimes they are surprised by their reactions, whether it is a positive reaction or negative. They may feel a sense of excitement and notice goosebumps or they may have a sense of anxiety or dread that they notice as a sinking feeling in the gut area. Sometimes they listen to these feelings and sometimes they don't. Continue to pay attention to the messages your body gives you and you'll soon find that you become more in tune with your body's responses. At the start it can be helpful to journal your impressions.

PAY ATTENTION TO YOUR THOUGHTS AND INNER VOICE

We talked earlier about noticing your thoughts. Sometimes a thought will pop into your mind out of the blue and hold special meaning; for example, my experience when looking for a new home of having a thought that was not characteristic of my usual ones. Or, when conducting therapy, a thought might pop into my mind that is on a different track to the current discussion but turns out to be pivotal. I have noticed these thoughts have a different nature — it is almost as though I am witnessing them. I have also found that a solution to a problem I have been pondering over can come into my mind some time later. For reasons such as this, it is important to pay attention to thoughts that enter your mind that are a bit different to your usual ones. My friend Gia told me a story of driving home one day and being at the traffic lights near her parents' house, when she heard her father's voice in her mind. She recognised that he needed assistance and so changed her route and went immediately to their house. Her father was not well and their phone line had suddenly died. They could not believe it when Gia walked in and was able to help them!

GUIDANCE THROUGH MEDITATION

Mindfulness and meditation have been referred to in earlier chapters as an important step in developing intuition. We can extend this to applying intuition in your everyday life. Apart from practising mindfulness or meditation each day, various teachers speak about asking for inner guidance in life through meditation. This can be helpful when you are seeking answers or exploring different directions in life. Whenever accessing your intuition, it is important to have a process of clearing and grounding.[103] The following meditation by Peirce involves a process of clearing and centring your focus, and grounding to the earth, as well as a sense of expansion.[104] Become familiar with this process so that you can use it or something similar at the start of any meditation.

MEDITATION ON LIGHT

Sit in a chair with your feet on the floor and your palms resting on your thighs. Close your eyes, breathe evenly and bring your attention inside your body. Draw the energy from above your head into the centre of your head. Imagine a point in the middle of your brain — let a pinprick of light break through right there. Through that white hole, allow light to emerge and form a small ball of light. Imagine the light radiating through your brain in all directions, clearing away old thoughts of fear, doubt and confusion.

Now shift your attention to the base of your spine and imagine a spot just in front of your tailbone. At that spot, let a second pinprick of light break through. Again, allow the light to emerge and form a small ball. Let the light spread, filling your pelvis with light.

Allow that light to drop straight down from the bottom of your spine into the earth below you. Watch it reaching down towards the centre of the earth, forming a column of clear light, merging into the clear light at the centre of the earth. Energy starts to rise up from the earth's core into your body. Feel the energy entering through the bottom of your feet and flowing up through your legs into the rest of your body.

When it comes to asking for inner guidance, Orloff suggests asking your mind in meditation, 'What do I need to be aware of or know right now?' Then notice the thoughts, feelings or images that appear. She points out that the response might be delayed; for example, you might be wondering about an issue and sometime later you come across an answer — in a TV program or book, or someone you know says something related to it and the answer comes to you.[105] I've certainly had that experience, both when working with clients and in my writing, particularly when looking for ideas or inspiration. An adaptation of Orloff's meditation on accessing your intuition follows.

ACCESSING YOUR INTUITION
MEDITATION

Make yourself comfortable in a quiet place and let your eyes close. Breathe and relax a little more with each breath out. Let your thoughts drift out of your mind, like clouds floating across the sky.

Centre and ground yourself then focus your awareness on the body. Allow your awareness to settle in the area of the solar plexus. Breathe into this area and deepen your sense of relaxation. As you breathe into this area, find a deep and quiet place within yourself. You naturally have access to your own intuitive guidance. As you rest deeply within yourself, get in touch with this inner wisdom. Ask it, 'What do I need to be aware of or know right now?' Be open to the response. You might have thoughts, images or feelings. Be receptive to them and accepting. Or you might just feel deeply relaxed right now, and the response will come later.

Again, when you are ready, notice your breath, gradually have a stretch and come back to the room.

Sometimes we want assistance in making decisions. We can ask the mind for guidance by using 'yes' or 'no' questions in meditation and noticing the feelings and images that come to mind. You might have the feeling of being pulled towards 'yes', perhaps with feelings of joy or relief. Images related to a 'yes' response might include flowers or a bird taking flight. Music might come to you. In contrast, a 'no' response might involve feelings of shutting down, numbness or a sense of dread.

Negative images such as an ominous storm or an airless room, or maybe a snippet of sombre music might signal 'no'.[106]

Rosanoff takes us through a meditation on getting in touch with 'yes' and 'no' responses in relation to a particular decision. Once you understand your responses, then you can ask for guidance in meditation. I have adapted Rosanoff's meditation here.[107]

'YES' OR 'NO' MEDITATION

Make yourself comfortable and let your eyes close. Take a few moments to focus on your breath and let each breath relax you more deeply. Allow your hands to rest on your lap, with your palms facing upwards.

Now think about the decision you need to make and imagine that in one hand you are holding the word 'yes', and in the other hand you holding the word 'no'. See the letters and feel their weight, sense their texture. Take a few moments to focus on the word 'yes'. How does it feel? How do you feel? Do any images or sounds come to mind? Now take a few moments on the word 'no'. How does it feel? How do you feel? Take as long as you would like to explore all the sensations, feelings, visions or music that go with the word 'no'.

When you have a clear sense of 'yes' and 'no', you might want to ask questions of your intuition in your mind and sense the response. Explore this idea for a while. Then, when you are ready, you can open your eyes and come back to the room.

When you are finished, take a few moments to breathe and think about what your intuition has been communicating to you about your decision. The ideomotor signals described earlier or pendulums work in similar ways and you might find these useful. Another meditation to assist with decision-making, based on different paths, is adapted here.[108]

PATH MEDITATION

Make yourself comfortable and let your eyes close. Breathe and relax and let go of the thoughts or distractions of the day. Imagine yourself walking down a path and feel the ground under your feet. Take a few moments to notice what is around you and notice that the weather is just right for you.

While you are walking, go over the decision you have to make in your mind and consider what the options are in relation to this decision. Then number them. You might have two options or even more. As you are walking, a little way ahead the path breaks up into several paths. It splits into as many paths as you have possibilities in relation to your decision. When you come to the place in the path where the road divides, stop for a moment and notice that each path represents one of your options. Number the paths in any direction that is comfortable for you and let those numbers correspond to the numbers of your possibilities.

Take your time and take a medium breath in and out. Then slowly travel down one of the paths. Notice how you feel. Where does the path take you and how comfortable are you on this path? Does it feel right? Take as long as you want to explore this path. When you have finished, go back to the place where the paths meet.

Choose another path and explore it as you did the first one. Continue exploring until you have experienced each path. When you have finished, take another medium breath in and out. Then, when you are ready, open your eyes, back in the room.

Now take a few moments to reflect on your meditation and what you experienced. Contemplate which path felt most 'right' to you.

WRITE

Another way to tap into intuition in our everyday life is to write. We talked earlier on about paying attention to our thoughts, feelings and sensations related to intuition and the usefulness of writing to heighten this awareness. You might keep a daily journal and record your experiences or reflect on life. You might want to make your journal special — perhaps by finding an attractive journal to use or decorating a notebook. At the start of your journal, you might consider writing about 'what you love'. According to Choquette, writing about this enables us to get in touch with our spirit.[109] Your journal is about you and your life, so I suggest reading your entry about what you love before you write in your journal each time, to open up your mind and spirit to joy and possibilities. Or consider doing a brief meditation before you write, clearing the mind and asking your intuition for guidance.

Several authors refer to writing as a means of accessing everyday intuition, either through journalling or by asking specific questions and then responding to them. You could write the questions that you want to address at the top of the page. These might relate to past events, work, money or relationships. Consider doing a short meditation and ask that you be guided by your intuition in your responses. Then go about answering the questions — trust what you write, just let the answers flow. You can ask about decisions in this way too. Some people ask the questions with their dominant hand and answer with their non-dominant hand as a way of accessing the intuitive and creative part of the mind.

APPLY INTUITION IN YOUR EVERYDAY AND WORKING LIFE

- Nurture your everyday intuition and listen to your body, as it gives valuable information about people, places and decisions.
- Pay attention to thoughts that pop into your mind or that are a bit different to your usual thoughts, as they may give you valuable information.
- We can access our intuition in meditation. There are specific meditations in which you ask your mind questions and there are meditations that can assist with decision-making.
- Journalling is another way of accessing your intuition. You can meditate before writing or ask questions and then respond to them.

DEVELOP TRUST

You might have noticed that the word trust has appeared a number of times in this text. The most important aspect of developing your intuition is developing trust in yourself and in your intuitive capabilities. This is the key to 'the secret garden' and the reason why trust sits right at the centre of our model on page 62, with the seven steps all stemming from it. How many times have you had a gut-feeling and not paid attention to it? I still get caught out! Those who are intuitive often differentiate 'head versus heart'. The former refers to use of the rational mind and logical thinking, and the 'heart' in this context refers to emotions and intuition. We must learn to listen to both and to trust rather than discard our intuition.

Several people whom I interviewed for the book emphasised this, in particular Liz, who practises as a psychic; Lynn, an art therapist; and Sandy, a Reiki Master and counsellor. Here are some of their comments regarding trust.

As a child Liz would have strong intuitive feelings, but she did not understand what they meant. She had a major accident at nineteen and a 'near death experience'. Since that time she has become more spiritual and has had psychic experiences. She now does psychic readings. Liz said, 'Everybody has intuition ... [the key is to] have confidence and trust.' We must *ask*, *trust* and *believe*.

When she was a child, Lynn would know when things were going to happen but others would not listen. She also had an accident at the age of seventeen and noticed that her intuitive abilities developed after that. Lynn now works intuitively as an art therapist and she has learnt to trust her feelings.

Sandy said that we are all basically intuitive, but we have to learn to listen to the information that presents. How you get in touch and reconnect with your intuition, and in what area of your life intuition manifests, is different for each individual. However, people become so busy in their lives that they ignore what their body is trying to tell them and become disconnected from their intuition.

The thing that very often gets in the way of trust is fear. It is a natural and protective part of being human, designed to keep us safe. However, it can stop us from doing things, including listening to our intuition. Intuition involves neutral thoughts or feelings, but our reaction to them can be fear. The aim is to defuse this fear, but to do this we need to understand ourselves and look at how the fear gets in the way of us expressing ourselves.[110]

Much of this book is about getting to know yourself better. Consider these questions: Has fear impacted on your ability to express yourself or listen to your intuition? Where does this fear come from? Why is it so hard to have faith in ourselves and our innate abilities? Well, we are influenced by society and all that it involves, including our family and our friends, our peers, education, religion, culture, media and government. Because of these influences, growing up in Australia is different (not better or worse, just different) from growing up in China or the United States. These influences shape our underlying beliefs about ourselves, the world and our future.

When you think about it, in our society we are taught to follow rules, to think logically and to achieve. Children are often intuitive and some are very sensitive. They might be told to stop being sensitive and 'develop a thick skin' to survive. The media constantly bombards us with images of trauma and destruction. We do need order in our society and logic but there can be a downside. We can retreat into fear, lose touch with our creative and intuitive sides, lose sight of our dreams and not believe in our own self. My son always loved drawing and painting when he was young and I was often setting up his easel and paints for him. He went to a fabulous school that encouraged him in many areas. By high school, however, he expressed that he did not enjoy art at all. Why was this? I wonder if it was because the classes were all about drawing techniques rather than expression. He was taught how to produce paintings using the skills of Picasso or Van Gogh, but what he sometimes wanted to do was to create his own.

I remember too that when my son was heading into his teenage years, a teacher asked him what he wanted to do when he finished school. He replied, 'I want to be a rock musician.' The teacher said that was not a career and he should think about something else. I couldn't resist and chipped in that it was great to have a dream and that if he wanted to pursue a career in music that was fine. Interestingly he is now pursuing his dream and studying to compose and perform his own music. He recently said, 'I don't know when it will happen, whether it is in one year, five years or ten, but I will have a band and travel the world.' I believe that he will.

Teacher and educational innovator Loris Malaguzzi describes beautifully how children are taught to not have dreams or be creative:

The child has a hundred ways of thinking ...
a hundred worlds to dream,
but they steal ninety-nine
the school and the culture[111]

As a result of such influences we can also develop a negative or critical voice in our mind, which perhaps says that we are not capable of different things, including being intuitive. We learn to look outside ourselves for answers (to experts) rather than within ourselves. In addition, we look outside ourselves for reinforcement and approval. So many of my clients refer to themselves as 'people-pleasers'. Can you relate to this?

As mentioned earlier, I find Cognitive Behaviour Therapy (CBT) very useful in my work. Based on the view that thoughts, feelings and behaviours are inter-related, CBT invites you to notice your feelings and your thoughts. We often mix up our feelings and our thoughts, perhaps saying, 'I *feel* as though I've made a mess of things.' This is actually a thought; the feeling might be sadness or disappointment.

We all have fairly constant streams of thoughts, often automatic in nature, which can impact on our feelings and behaviours. In CBT, the therapist works together with the client to guide them through strategies such as identifying which thoughts are helpful and which are unhelpful, and then learning to challenge and correct the unhelpful ones. In addition, underlying beliefs are examined.[112] A number of unhelpful unconscious beliefs drive our thoughts. Such beliefs include that we need to be loved and approved of by everyone or need to be highly competent at everything (the basis of perfectionism) or perhaps in control all of the time. These beliefs work for us in some ways, in that we aim to do our best and put in effort to achieve, but it is not possible to fulfil them perfectly all of the time, and so they can also push us around in negative ways.

Through my work in this area, I have often reflected on my own thinking and underlying beliefs. My beliefs have helped me to achieve my aim of being of service to people, but there have been costs. At times I have given myself a hard time for not always achieving my very high expectations. I've also worked far too hard at times, exhausting myself mentally and physically in the process. I reflected once on where these beliefs came from in my life and I found myself thinking about being six years old at school. Each Friday we had a test and we would then be put in order of our results for the following week. Those who did well would be placed at the back of the room and those who did poorly were placed at the front! On one occasion I was sick and missed the test; I was very upset at being put at the front of the class the following week!

We need to trust in ourselves and let go of our expectations. We know ourselves very well (better than anyone else) and we have many innate abilities, including intuition. So let go of any doubts or negative thoughts and *trust* your intuition.

To begin this process, Peirce suggests that we:

- Write down our fears or what we feel negative about and see if these are focused on the past.
- Replace the words in the statements with positive and loving words, such as acceptance and forgiveness.

Consider how our actions might be different with this more positive outlook, what our actions would be and how outcomes might be different.[113]

Let's use the steps above to work through an example.

Step 1: *My boss upset me — I applied for a pay rise and she said she could not see any reasons for it. She does not recognise the value in what I have been working on. This isn't the first time in my life where I have not felt valued.*

Step 2: *She has a different background and worldview. What she sees as important is not what I see as important. I can accept this and let go of the old hurt.*

Step 3: *What is important is that I recognise the value of my work and my own self.*

Rebecca Rosen, author and intuitive, has suggested another useful exercise for letting go of fears that could easily be adapted to intuition. She suggests aligning the following affirmations in your mind with each breath out:

Affirm on the first breath: 'I am willing to let go of all past thoughts and fears that are holding me back.'

On the second breath: 'I am willing to let go of all my thoughts and fears that keep me from being fully present.'

On the third breath, 'I am willing to let go of all future fears and anxieties that may stand in my way of becoming all that I am meant to be.'[114]

I regularly refer to the following meditation with clients when we are working together on developing a greater sense of self-worth or when they perceive that there are issues for them to let go of (such as some of the beliefs mentioned above). Again, you might like to try the following meditation and apply it to your intuition.

INSTILLING POSITIVES AND LETTING GO OF NEGATIVES MEDITATION

Make yourself comfortable and let your eyes close. Focus on the breath and relax. Using all of your senses, imagine being in the countryside or at the beach. Find a spot to sit or stand near the water, and notice there are some pebbles or shells on the ground around you. Gather some of them up and feel them in your hand, see their colours and feel their textures.

Your mind is like the water: the surface is like the conscious part of the mind; underneath the surface is like the unconscious.

Now take your time and attach positive meaning to each of the pebbles or shells. One might represent confidence or trust in your intuitive abilities; another might represent looking after yourself. Then, one by one, toss them into the water. Know that they will penetrate the surface of the water and float down until they settle on the bottom. In the same way, these ideas will settle into your mind.

A small distance away is a sailing boat tethered to the shore by a rope. This is not a boat to go sailing in. It is for you to use to let go of any negatives you choose to. On the sand are some sponges and pieces of driftwood. Gather some up and, this time, to each attach something you would like to let go of: perhaps self-doubt, inaction or fear. Then toss each one into the boat. When you are finished, untie the rope and toss it into the boat. Magically the boat will sail far away, where it need not be of any concern to you.

You have instilled positives into your mind and let go of what you want to. When you are ready, gradually open your eyes and return to the here and now.

How was the meditation? What did you choose to instil in your mind? What did you let go of?

TRUST

- At the heart of developing your intuition lies developing trust in yourself and in your intuitive capabilities.
- Fear can get in the way, perhaps originating from influences growing up, leading to self-criticism.
- We need to be aware of our thinking, unhelpful beliefs and self-doubt.
- We need to work on challenging those thoughts and reframing them, and we need to let go of self-doubt and fear.
- Take a leap of faith and trust yourself and your intuition.

REFLECTIONS

This part of the book has been focused on the how of intuition. I have given you a series of steps or strategies to raise your awareness of and to enhance your intuition. These included making space for intuition through clutter-clearing, mindfulness and meditation. We looked at ways to raise self-awareness and to develop creativity. Accessing and listening to the unconscious mind, and allowing guidance by your inner wisdom, is an important step. Part of the process is showing compassion to others and yourself, focusing on gratitude, and your passion and purpose in life. I have encouraged you to apply intuition in your everyday life. The more you do this, the more your intuition will improve. Most importantly, remember that central to intuition is trust. So many times we doubt ourselves and our intuition, but when we trust our heart and mind, our intuition can blossom!

Your 'intuition garden' journal

In your journal, write down your response to the following questions:
1. Which ideas in this middle part of the book resonated with you most?
2. What steps do you think you want to continue to work on?

PART 3

PHENOMENA RELATED TO INTUITION

The intuitive mind is a Sacred Gift and the rational mind is a faithful servant. We have created a society that honours the servant and has forgotten the gift.

ALBERT EINSTEIN

We have been busy in the intuition garden in the first two parts of this book! Let's imagine now that the garden is just about complete — and it's beautiful. There are plenty of peaceful spots for you to linger in, so choose one of your favourites and sit down and relax. In this section we are going to reflect on some of the phenomena related to intuition. These are fascinating and may well give you more ideas for your 'intuition garden'. In clinical practice, we often seed ideas into people's minds then see if they settle in and grow. So let's seed a few more ideas now and see what happens with them! In this final section we will consider a number of related topics, namely synchronicity, premonitions and the third eye. We will also focus on healing, as intuition can play an integral role in this field.

Chapter 5

SYNCHRONICITY, PREMONITIONS AND THE THIRD EYE

If it happens, it is possible.

AN UNNAMED LAW OF THE UNIVERSE

Synchronicity refers to the coincidences we sometimes experience when everything seems to fall seamlessly into place. Premonitions give us glimpses of the future. And it is via our 'third eye' that we can gain greater access to our inner world and our intuition. By understanding these phenomena and being aware of them, we can help our intuition garden to flourish.

SYNCHRONICITY

I have been fascinated by the phenomenon of synchronicity for many years. Deepak Chopra refers to intuition as 'the gateway to synchronicity', and highlights the role of coincidence in shaping our lives. He wisely says, 'Even when you think you have your life all mapped out, things happen that shape your destiny in ways you might never even have imagined.'[1] I imagine that in the year 2000, Mary Donaldson had a certain map of her life in her mind. Perhaps it involved work and travel. However, all that changed the night she met Crown Prince Frederik of Denmark in a Sydney pub! Today, as Crown Princess Mary of Denmark, her life is probably very different from anything she could have imagined back then.

Synchronicity needn't always be so spectacularly life changing, however. For example, how often does it happen that we need to deal with an issue or problem in life and we spot an article in a magazine or a book containing just the right information or advice? We have all experienced coincidences in our lives. I can remember quite a few, some more significant than others. When I was a medical student, I drove to Melbourne (800 kilometres away) in my blue mini for a student placement. On my way back, a familiar car drove past me and the person inside waved. I realised that it was a friend from medical school and I waved back. A few minutes later, my car overheated and stopped, about 20 kilometres out of the nearest town. I quickly got out and checked the situation — my radiator was steaming. These were the days before mobile phones. I was just working out what to do next when my friend reappeared. He had noticed that my mini had disappeared from his rear-view mirror and so he had turned around and come back to check on me. He kindly towed me into the next town where I had my car fixed before heading on my way again. Quite uncanny that my friend appeared at just the right moment!

Another amazing set of coincidences occurred prior to writing my second book. I had invited a speaker to a workshop I was hosting and wanted to have his books on hand at my practice. So I emailed the publisher to ask if I could get hold of some stock. She emailed back and said that she noticed from my signature that

I worked at a certain university and (at the time) taught on the counselling program. She apologised for then putting my name into Google, where she'd discovered that I had written a book on depression. Would I like to talk about writing more books? And now, here we are working on a third book together. Lucky for me that her intuition was working!

Some might ask if these occurrences just aren't purely random. I think they're more than that. Chopra comments that, 'When you live your life with an appreciation of coincidences and their meanings, you connect with the underlying field of infinite possibilities.'[2] It also seems that the way to experience more synchronicity is to become more aware of coincidences and pay more attention to them. One way of doing this is to record in your journal the synchronicities that are happening in your life. Another way is to spend a few minutes at the end of each day reviewing it.[3]

REVIEWING DAILY COINCIDENCES MEDITATION

Make yourself comfortable and let your eyes close. Take a few breaths in and out and imagine that you are watching a TV or computer screen and reviewing the day. You have the controls and you are going to focus on coincidences that occurred during the day.

Imagine you're watching a film of your day, from start to finish, noticing any synchronicities. Be curious too about the related messages that come into your mind, and remember to trust the message.

Spend as long as you want watching the film. Then, when you are ready, open your eyes and return to the room.

A further meditation aimed at raising awareness of coincidences requires you to remember the past five years. However, it is not advisable to do this exercise if you do not think that you will feel comfortable doing so.[4] Pay attention to the coincidences that you discover.

REMEMBERING COINCIDENCES MEDITATION

Make yourself comfortable and let your eyes close. Think about what you have been doing over the past 24 hours. Move backwards from the here and now through your memory to where you were one day previously. Identify details about what you were doing, what you were thinking and feeling.

Choose a theme from the past day and focus on it. Then gradually think back to five years ago. Go back year by year until you reach the same date five years ago. Where were you? What were you doing? Get a clear image of life at that time. Then track this theme over the past five years back to the present. Pay attention to what comes to mind. When you are ready, gradually open your eyes and reorientate to the here and now.

SYNCHRONICITY

- Coincidence is linked with intuition, and shapes our lives.
- We can enhance our awareness of synchronicity through meditation and journalling.
- Opening up to synchronicity in our lives opens our lives up to more possibilities.

PREMONITIONS

A premonition is defined as an intuition about the future or a feeling that something is about to happen, especially something unpleasant; a forewarning or a glimpse of the future.[5] Premonitions come in many different forms and may be vague feelings or dramatic visions. They may occur while we are asleep or awake. Humans have been fascinated by premonitions since ancient times. Nearly all cultures have regarded 'the heart as a conduit to a source of information and wisdom lying beyond the reach of the physical senses, whether called intuition or premonitions'.[6] And in 1882, the Society for Psychical Research was established in the United Kingdom to conduct research into human experiences such as premonitions that challenged contemporary scientific models.

Paranormal researcher Larry Dossey reports that it is a common experience for doctors to know when they are about to be called in for obstetric deliveries; they may be on their way when they are summoned. He 'envision[s] a day when our medical schools honour our distant connections and teach young physicians and nurses how to cultivate them, then the healing professions will be transformed and humanised'.[7] Judith

Orloff is now teaching medical students about intuition in the United States. Maybe we will follow this example in Australia. Many clinicians I know are aware of using their intuition in their work, but they often need a sense of 'permission' to use it.

Dean Radin, a parapsychology researcher from California, has found that our nervous system automatically responds to events that have not yet happened and of which we are unaware. He calls this 'presentiment', described as a vague non-cognitive sense that something good or bad will occur.[8] A 'premonition centre' in the brain has not been identified, but research is suggesting that the hippocampus may be involved.[9] Researchers suggest that we should emphasise 'whole-body knowing', rather than just the brain being involved.[10] The ability to know distant events is often called 'second sight' and is seen as a fundamental ability that everyone has. One of the reasons why premonitions might have evolved is that those humans who possess 'second sight' had a survival advantage over those who did not.[11]

It has been proposed that some of the factors that make us likely to have premonitions are:[12]

- Comfort with the world of imagination.
- Belief in the transcendent.
- A sense of the unity of all life, and seeing oneself as part of a web of relationships.
- Compassion and empathy, leading to connectedness with others.
- High levels of intuition.
- Comfort with unexpected patterns in life.
- Finding meaning in life.
- Interest and positivity.
- Respect for the unconscious.
- Intuitive personality type.

Premonitory dreams have already been mentioned in Chapter 4, and I described a particular dream that I had many years ago. Since that time, I have had several other dreams that I believe involved premonitions. One of my sisters was due to travel to the United Kingdom when I was in my early twenties. Just before she left, I dreamt of a plane flying directly into a mountain peak. I awoke, shaken by the realism of the dream, and asking myself whether this was my sister's plane, should I say anything, was it nothing or was it something important? In the end, I felt that she was safe and did not say anything to worry her. She left and arrived safely in the UK. However, a day or so later an aircraft flew directly into Mt Erebus in Antarctica and everyone onboard was killed.

Another dream relating to a disaster happened on the night of the Thredbo landslide in New South Wales in 1997. I had gone to bed with my then-husband about 10 p.m. and fell asleep, then found myself dreaming that I was walking on a mountain road with a family friend. We had recently met up with him and he told us about a skiing trip he had just returned from. In my dream there was a sudden landslide. I awoke and sat up, feeling as if the ground was literally shaking. I actually woke up my husband and told him what I had dreamt. It was about 11 p.m. When I listened to the news the next morning, I discovered there had been a terrible landslide at Thredbo at about 11.30 p.m. The time difference between New South Wales and my state would have been about half an hour.

During the interviews for this book, a number of individuals talked about premonitions:

Rosie sometimes has flashes of particular things that are going to happen in people's lives when she passes them in the street. She also had the experience when visiting a friend of knowing that the friend was going to become very sick and die. The friend was soon after diagnosed with terminal leukaemia.

Julie experienced intuition about her first husband. Before there was even an inkling that he was mentally unwell, she drove past a private psychiatric hospital and knew that he would be admitted there. She was right. Sadly, Julie also had a premonition that he was dead on the day he passed away.

Natalie was happily married and pregnant with her second child when she had strong feelings that something was going to go wrong. She and her husband talked about this feeling. It wouldn't leave her, even though the early pregnancy tests were all okay. Towards the end of the pregnancy, her husband became acutely unwell and died very quickly of leukaemia. Her intuitive feelings had been about him.

Mel had a dream two years ago about her grandmother that was very vivid. She had the feeling that her grandmother had died and she awoke feeling distraught. The next day Mel received a phone call from her mother that her grandmother had had a seizure and was in hospital. She had been unresponsive when the ambulance arrived and was not expected to live. Fortunately, 24 hours later it became evident that she would pull through.

PREMONITIONS

- Refers to intuition about the future or a forewarning, often called 'second sight'.
- Medical practitioners often report premonitions and there is growing interest in 'clinical intuition'.
- Premonitions may occur as visions or feelings, or in dreams.

THE THIRD EYE

The concept of the third eye was introduced in Chapter 1. It is not fully understood, but then again, we don't fully understand the mind and how it works. In the spiritual world, the third eye is viewed as the portal to access the different levels of consciousness, including your Higher Self or potentially a Higher Power. It can help us perceive beyond our regular senses. It is used by energy healers and clairvoyants, and it can also be a part of our regular meditation practices. There are many meditations based on the third eye, mostly arising from Eastern approaches, and at times relating to meditations on the chakras (as outlined on page 101). If you feel comfortable to try a meditation related to the third eye, then the following meditation can help you to become aware of it.[13]

SENSING THE THIRD EYE MEDITATION

Sit with your eyes closed and lower your chin to your chest. Look gently upwards with your eyes closed, as if you are looking out through the centre of your forehead, just above the eyes. Notice any colours or any images of an eye that come into your mind. Continue to breathe and relax. Open your eyes when you are ready.

What did you sense in your mind? You might like to practise this meditation a number of times before moving onto the next one. Sometimes there are fears related to using the third eye, so you may want to look into this area more before going on to further meditations. The meditation below is one I have adapted; it draws on light and the chakras, and it helps us to feel more confident with the third eye.[14, 15]

MEDITATION ON THE THIRD EYE

Make yourself comfortable, let your eyes close, and focus your attention on the point between the eyebrows. Focus on the breath, take a few deep breaths in and out, then take a few moments to be aware of sensations arising from around you and in the body. Let go of any fear or uncertain thoughts. Feel safe and comfortable. Be aware of a sense of light from the top of your head entering your body and spreading through the whole body, extending down into the earth and back again to you through your feet.

Focus your attention on the interconnected energy system in your body and in turn on each chakra. See them as spinning discs:

- The root chakra, at the base of the spine, which is red.
- The sacral chakra, below the navel, which is orange.
- The solar plexus, which is yellow.
- The heart chakra, behind the heart, which is green.
- The throat chakra, where the neck meets the shoulders, which is cobalt blue.
- The third eye, in the forehead, which is indigo blue sometimes with flashes of light.
- The crown chakra, just under the top of the skull, which is purple.

Move to the third eye again and focus more intently on it. Notice a ball of light emanating from it. Your third eye allows you to see within when your two eyes are closed.

It is your consciousness and it is radiating golden light in all directions. Allow the light to flow through you and out through the third eye. Surround yourself with this light and allow it to fill your entire body. If you choose to, and if you sense you have guides, you can ask them to support you and to help you to connect with your Higher Self. There may be a message about opening your third eye, or other messages. Notice any images or impressions that come to mind.

Take your time. Then, when you are ready, in your mind see your third eye close. Gradually return to the room, fully present and in the here and now.

How did you find this meditation? It might be one that you choose to do regularly or you might like to attend a meditation class that incorporates work with the third eye so that you can explore this phenomenon further.

THE THIRD EYE

- Is referred to as the portal to the different levels of your consciousness, including your Higher Self.
- We can open it through meditation practice.

REFLECTIONS

This chapter has certainly taken us in some interesting directions. As I wrote it, all my experiences related to synchronicities and premonitions came to mind. Do you have space in your intuition garden for synchronicities or premonitions, or are you keen to explore the concept of the third eye further? Perhaps these notions already exist in your garden or perhaps they will seed in your mind and grow.

Your 'intuition garden' journal

In your journal, write down your answers to the following questions:

1. What ideas can you take away from this chapter?
2. How can you incorporate these ideas into your life?

Chapter 6

HEALING

*If the head and body are to be well, you must begin
by curing the soul. That is the first thing.*

PLATO

A key reason for writing about the topic of intuition has been to explore its role in healing. Healing has been touched on in many ways throughout this book — the art of healing, empathy, the healing power of loving-kindness, suggestion and hypnosis, and hands-on healing such as Reiki. With healing we must respect rational knowledge but also harness our own deeper inner wisdom, our intuition. If we relate the concept of healing and intuition to our garden, let's imagine our garden is now established and very beautiful, but the wonderful thing about gardens is that they are always changing and there is so much potential for further change. So if we enhance our intuition garden with healing, it will flourish even more and assist us in healing ourselves and others.

HEALING AND INTUITION

When you look into the role of intuition in healing, you find that many forms of traditional medicines (ancient Greek, Indian, Tibetan, Chinese) utilise herbs and natural compounds to heal disease. The question arises of how these remedies were devised, and the answer is via intuition. For example, in the Tibetan Buddhist tradition, the Medicine Buddha tells the practitioner what substances to use. In the case of Native Americans, it is said that the plant tells the healer what it is good for.[1] Modern medicine is based on science but intuition has also played a role in medical discovery through the generation of ideas to study and directions to follow.

Gia spoke to me of an experience that she had when she was diagnosed with breast cancer at the age of 33. She was lying in her hospital bed, listening to the surgeons telling her what procedures and treatments she needed to consider. For a few moments, however, she lost her hearing. Then she heard a voice in her head saying loud and clear, 'Let them do whatever they want. What are you going to do about your life?'

After this message, her hearing returned and she turned to the doctors and said, 'I will have it all [the medical treatments].' But she knew that she also had to change her life. Since then she has recovered and thrived, reconnected with her intuition and transformed her working life to healing through counselling and therapeutic touch.

Jennifer Berlingieri, an art therapy student, carried out research into the experience of using intuition in art therapy. She wanted to explore how intuition informed her practice and how to integrate intuition into her practice. The project required her to follow her creativity and intuition as she worked on an exhibition. She was guided by her intuitive thoughts, such as, 'Make the art first ... all the essences that need to be expressed will come out in the making.' She also looked for moments in her professional life that felt intuitive and she soon became aware that intuition informed her more regularly than she'd thought. She spoke of an intuitive space in an art therapy session involving both her intuitive knowing and that of the client, in which they connected and found meaning.[2]

Over the years, I have learnt to listen to my intuition in practice. This began as an Occupational Therapist; then in my early years as a hospital doctor and later in general practice and therapy. Intuition might involve a gut-feeling that there is a serious problem (related to physical illness or suicidal tendencies), or it might become evident through a thought that enters my mind and becomes a turning point in the process. A number of my colleagues have had the same experience and incorporate intuition into their practice. Not long ago there was an article in the newspaper about midwives. A number were interviewed for the article and one said that the key thing she had learnt over the years as a midwife was that 'the woman knows; you need to trust her intuition'.[3] Some individuals are medical intuitives, able to use their intuition to pick up health issues and also advise or use healing techniques.

So how can intuition be incorporated into therapy? For some individuals, such as Lynn, an art therapist, intuition begins with meditation prior to the arrival of a client. In the meditation, Lynn tunes into any intuitive information about the individual or the key issue to work on in the session. Other therapists, such as Heather, connect with the individual in the first minutes of the session and listen to their own intuitive thoughts and feelings directing them regarding what to focus on in the session. Hands-on therapists (such as Sandy who practises Reiki) pick up information as they treat the person and let it guide them on where in the body to focus their healing.

In my own practice, I believe intuition comes into play from the moment I hear a client on the phone or see them in person. As mentioned earlier, relationships are central to our lives, whether with loved ones, work colleagues or a therapist. From the first moment, I am aiming to establish a connection with the individual and to develop trust and rapport. The essence of therapy work is the therapeutic relationship. Unless there is a trusting connection between therapist and client, the individual will not gain from therapy.

When someone comes into my rooms, I observe them from as soon as I see or hear them, noticing their appearance, how they stand and walk, how they talk. Observation of non-verbal behaviours (such as eye contact and movements, signs of nervousness or distress) is integral to the process. I endeavour to be fully present or mindful when with an individual in therapy, and this naturally leads to a more non-judgmental stance. This comes more easily when I am feeling grounded in myself from the outset of the therapy session. As soon as the person begins talking, I actively listen to them, tuning into their exact words and the emotion expressed in the words as well as the non-verbal behaviours.

In therapy, I get a sense of the person's energy, whether they seem anxious, tired or depressed, or positive or peaceful, for example. I have learnt to notice feelings within myself, both sensations within my body as well as my thoughts and emotions. Thinking might be related to processing the information provided to me by the client or intuitive thoughts might simply pop into my mind. I regularly check with the individual whether these thoughts fit with them. All this information helps to guide the session.

It is always important in therapy to hear and understand

the person's story or narrative. We all want to be heard and understood, and every person's story is unique. Part of the early phase of therapy is exploring the individual's values and it is from these that we understand how the person perceives the world. Understanding values enables us to create meaningful goals together to move towards change. As I mentioned early on in the book, I practise multimodal therapy, incorporating a range of approaches. Deciding on which approach or approaches to utilise involves a combination of knowledge, experience, creativity and intuition. My underlying aim is to take a holistic approach, addressing all areas in life, including the spiritual if appropriate to the individual.

There are also times in the therapy session when the therapist and the client are connected and communicating well, when moments of clarity and intuition and healing occur. It was Carl Rogers, a humanistic psychologist who developed person-centred therapy, who said that when he was closest to his intuitive self, 'when perhaps I am in a slightly altered state of consciousness … whatever I do seems to be full of healing'.[4] These words resonate with me and describe particular moments in therapy beautifully. The 'slightly altered state of consciousness' reference is interesting. This seems to occur when the therapist is paying attention fully, in the moment, and as a result goes into a mindful or hypnotic state. It is in this state of mind that intuitive experiences can result.

Returning to the concepts of the brain and the mind, psychiatrist Dan Siegel has written a series of fascinating books on the brain and on mindfulness in particular. In one of his books, *The Mindful Therapist*, Siegel refers to holistic practice and reports that the words 'holistic', 'healing' and 'health' are all derived from 'whole', that is, we are 'part of an interdependent whole'. He goes on to convey the message that if we are part of the interconnected flow of life, we have a powerful role in helping others and healing the planet, beginning with ourselves.[5] He refers to this sense of interconnection as 'transpiration'.

Siegel provides the acronym PART for holistic practice, where:

'P' stands for presence, involving being grounded in oneself, open to others and participating fully in the life of the mind.

'A' refers to attunement; that is, tuning into the incoming streams of information. This involves being fully attuned to what is being sent rather than becoming influenced by one's own preconceived ideas or biases. Siegel talks about 'mindsight' skills, or perceiving the interior of our body (interoception), in relation to attunement. Mindsight is akin to the sixth sense and attunement relies on it.[6]

'R' is for resonance, the physiological result of presence and attunement, and the alignment of two beings into a functional whole. In this aligned state, each person influences the internal state of the other. This is associated with feeling safe and secure (essential to the therapeutic relationship).[7]

'T' relates to the 'trust' that develops when we have resonance with someone; 'truth', experienced as we open up to others and ourselves; 'tracking', or the process of tracking information flow between people, which can set the scene for our innate drive for 'neural integration', and which allows us to be less rigid (more flexible) and experience a sense of harmony; and for 'training', as 'the brain is like a muscle' requiring mental exercise![8] 'T' also relates to 'transformation', the aim of therapy. Integral to this is neuroplasticity, the process of change in the structural connections in the brain in response to experience.

Siegel focuses on the centrality of mindfulness, mindsight and neural integration in assisting us towards health.[9] The psychological, social and biological aspects of the individual are all considered, and energy and information are seen to flow between them. Siegel speaks of the brain (the nervous system throughout the whole body), the mind (which regulates flow of information) and relationship (the way energy and information are shared), and he views mindsight as essential to shaping the internal world and to track energy and information flow within us and between us.[10] The aim of all of this is to move toward flexibility, harmony and integration.

There is growing interest in the role of intuition in therapy with recent neurobiology highlighting the role of the unconscious mind in 'clinical intuition'. Experienced therapists utilise implicit knowledge that is housed in the non-dominant brain. Clinical intuition involves sensing what is happening behind the client's words and beyond conscious awareness.[11] It is seen as filling the gap between theory and practice. Clinical intuition is necessary for deep change during psychotherapy.[12] Psychologist Marks-Tarlow throws light on the role of intuition in accessing implicit knowledge and the unconscious mind, and the importance of empathy, creativity, humour and compassion. She lists five characteristics of clinical intuition as being 'sudden recognition or immediate knowledge, emergent awareness, non-verbal insight (such as in dreams) and holisitic, integrative sensibilities'.[13]

Marks-Tarlow speaks of adopting an open and curious frame of mind, being grounded in inner sensory emotional and imaginative faculties, and receiving information consciously to prepare the mind for deeper connections to the client. This is described as a 'being with' rather than 'doing to' mode of interaction.[14] She also reports that these processes capitalise on brain plasticity. My experience of psychotherapy as being a creative process correlates with hers, as does the notion that there is a constant process of moving between right- and left-brain functions but the intuitive right side integrates the whole.[15]

She suggests six ways to set the foundation for intuitive awareness:[16]

1. Practise focus (through yoga, meditation, quiet sitting).

2. Open up your receptivity to inner emotional, sensory and body-based cues.

3. Develop a ritual for clearing, grounding and consulting your intuition; for example, the meditation on accessing your intuition on page 135.

4. Contact your inner signals; for example, pay attention to your body during a session with a client, without analysing what is happening.

5. Clarify your values as a clinician.

6. Set intentions for yourself; for example, healing, empathising, being authentic.

Developing intuitive awareness

In your journal, if you are a clinician, reflect on your values and your intentions in your practice. If you are not a clinician, what are your values and intentions in relation to your work or family life?

The work in the areas of mindfulness, mindsight and clinical intuition is incredibly exciting, as are the applications to practice. A number of authors, such as Deepak Chopra and Judith Orloff challenge us to consider intuition beyond neurobiology. Chopra describes intuition as 'an intelligence beyond the rational' and goes on to say that there are many answers within us and that with intuition we tap into 'the universal mind'. He sees that there are no barriers between us, there is the potential for an endless flow of information and energy, and that this flow is outside of space and time. Chopra acknowledges that this view requires a letting go or leap of faith, but it is a path to meaning and purpose.[17]

An inspiring client who is dealing with a connective tissue disease introduced me to the work of scientist David Hamilton. The driving force behind his work is the connection between the body, the mind and the spiritual. He explores how these connections might be involved in healing, from visualisation of movement in a limb that has lost power to the placebo effect of treatments. With both of these, improvements at a physical level can be made; for example, a placebo painkiller might trigger the production of endorphins, a natural painkilling substance in the body.[18]

Hamilton suggests that we take the leap of faith and accept that the mind can contribute to improvements in health or healing. One of the factors he identifies is positive attitude, which has been linked to improved immune system functioning, assisting us to fight illness. He cites studies on heart disease showing that a positive outlook is related to a reduced likelihood of developing heart disease.[19] One study reported in Hamilton's book stood out for me as it was set in general practice. Patients were given either a positive consultation (told what was wrong and that they would be better in a few days) or a negative consultation (not sure what was wrong). Several weeks later, Hamilton explains, a significant percentage of patients who had had a positive consultation had improved as opposed to a much lower percentage of patients who had had a negative consultation. In fact, the positive consultation was about twice as beneficial.[20]

Hamilton also reminds us of the life and writings of Viktor Frankl, who survived a Nazi concentration camp during World War II and taught us that, no matter what the circumstances, no one can take away our sense of meaning.[21] He refers to work around neuroplasticity of the brain and how studying a particular subject can result in many new nerve pathways being developed in relation to this area.[22] As part of this brain-changing process, neurotransmitters or nerve messenger chemicals are produced. Other substances, including proteins, are produced that help to switch on genetic material and create the new nerve pathways.[23] These proteins, or neuropeptides, are produced in the brain and travel around the body. They are associated with different states of mind including emotions or attitudes. The more these proteins are produced, the more 'receptors' on nerve cells (like a docking port to receive the protein) are also produced. Take as an example the feeling of frustration: the more thoughts related to frustration and the more neuropeptides that are produced, the more the receptors and the more we experience the emotion.[24] The converse is true: the more we experience calm, the more the connections alter. This is why practising meditation or having regular massage or Reiki can bring about lasting effects over time.

This is where visualisation comes in as well. When I watched the movie *Shine* recently, I noticed that David Helfgott would practise the very difficult and intricate pieces in his mind and the finger movements *away* from the piano until they became automatic (the nerve pathways were created). He would then let the emotion flow into his hands. In the same way, high-level athletes are trained to visualise their events. Studies have shown that visualising movements improves performance; that is, brain growth is enhanced.[25] It's why you often hear comments about the 'focus' of athletes at the Olympics and similar competitions. They are preparing themselves for their event by seeing themselves successfully navigate it in their mind.

Guided imagery or visualisation has been used in hypnotherapy for many years for relaxation and pain-relief and to bring about healing. It's been shown to improve respiratory function and quality of life in individuals with lung disease and also assist in wound healing. The release of cortisol, one of the hormones produced in the body as a result of stress, can be reduced with guided imagery, helping to thereby reduce the detrimental effects of stress.[26] Hamilton explains that the key to visualisation for healing is to imagine the process occurring in the body — focusing your attention on the diseased area activates the related part of the brain. He proposes that healing through genetic and chemical changes in the body and mind can occur.[27]

In guided imagery, a range of imagery can assist the individual to manage diseases such as cancer. For example, images such as a cancer tumour becoming smaller or melting away might be used. Alternatively, the patient might be encouraged to visualise the cancer surrounded by healing cells or being targeted by heat or light. Some individuals imagine themselves shrinking down in size until they can go inside the body and fight the cancer. If visualisation is difficult, other senses can be used. Hypnotherapists work with the unconscious mind to explore what the body needs or they might incorporate spiritual suggestions if these are relevant to the person. I recently worked with a woman who had been told she had a very nasty and aggressive cancer. She naturally became fearful of the cancer so we worked on ways of viewing it differently and harnessing her own power to focus on healing.

Affirmations can also be encouraged to instil positive thoughts and attitudes in patients. Sir Ken Robinson, education academic and author, makes reference to affirmations such as 'I am glowing with health, every cell is healthy and well.'[28] If you are interested in the area of physical healing in particular, I would recommend that you read Robinson's book *The Element*, as he has developed visualisations down to cellular and DNA level. He speaks of the vibrations of disease being replaced by stillness and then suggests waves of healing. Throughout his book there are stories of individuals managing illness and some wonderful ideas for visualisations. In pain management, for example, psychotherapy and hypnotherapy can be very effective — observing the pain, struggling less with the pain, relaxing generally, and changing the experience or image of the pain can all be helpful.

Orloff, in her writing, focuses on intuitive healing, describing it as integrative or respecting the intelligence of the rational mind, and calls on our inner wisdom to guide us. She writes that intuition takes us into the realm of possibilities 'even when science deems it impossible', and that this involves trust and being true to ourselves.[29] Five steps to intuitive healing are described by Orloff:

Notice your beliefs (conscious and unconscious), such as 'I am not worthy', as these influence the body. Do your beliefs give you strength during an illness? How do you treat yourself when you are sick, and can you be more compassionate? Orloff suggests adopting empowering beliefs, such as 'My path is perfect, I don't have to compare myself to anyone. I have the power to heal from hurt.'[30]

Be in your body to receive intuitive information (refer to Chapters 4 and 6).

Sense your body's inner energy, through awareness and meditation or perhaps by seeing a practitioner who works with chakras or Reiki.[31]

Ask for inner guidance through meditation: 'What does my gut say? Does it feel right or not? Does going ahead give me a sense of peace?' Orloff gives the example of asking a question such as, 'How can I prevent the headaches from occurring?' and then waiting for the response to come into the mind. You might feel pulled to the correct answer or get a sinking feeling if it's not correct. She also suggests connecting with the body and the breath then asking the body, 'What do you want to tell me at this time?'[32]

Pay attention to your dreams (as explained in Chapter 6) through awareness and journalling, and perhaps asking a question before bed and writing down the response in the morning. Orloff gives an example from her own life of asking about recurrent sinus infections. In her dream she saw herself at an acupuncturist's office, so she knew how to treat the problem![33]

My experience is that many of these steps can be helpful when working with others. Orloff gives an example from her own practice to which I can relate. On first meeting a particular client, she observed his body language and appearance but her sense went beyond these to feeling a sadness in the upper abdomen or solar plexus area and what felt like a yearning for what was past. Orloff also had the thought, 'Why can't I lead the life I imagined?' — all of this occurred before she had shaken hands with him. Orloff worked with him to feel more real and connected with his true self. He rediscovered his love of literature and poetry and felt a significant shift in his life as a result.

One of the ways that I look after myself is to see a colleague from time to time to work through issues or to experience healing. Seeing a psychic like Liz is a healing experience, as she shares her insights in a kind, caring and positive way. Given that I work with people in therapy for most of the week, I regularly enjoy a massage or Reiki session as a way of caring for myself and nurturing my spirit. I find it interesting what my friend Sandy says about her practice of Reiki, as this involves a healing and intuitive process. Since taking her Reiki Mastership, Sandy has found that her intuition has become stronger and more visual. Her intention is to be of service: 'The more I give, the more I receive. In Reiki when working on a client, I see information in my mind's eye, and feel energy flow through my hands. I sense information in a diversity of ways.'

Sandy said that she centres herself, entering a relaxed state of oneness with the universe and with the client, inviting the Reiki energy to flow. The intent is for the client to heal themselves. Her focus remains in the present moment with the client. In doing so, she is more able to actively listen and be intuitive. This intuition is reflected in the hand positions that are used, how long she holds a position, and also what is explored through conversation. As the treatment progresses the energy flows as does the information that is shared. A number of clients have been astounded by how much Sandy 'knows' about them.

Sandy says, 'Reiki was described to me by own Reiki Master as being in communion with another person. For this to happen one must be connected intuitively. I also draw on my intuition during counselling. It is not something that can be separated out from who I am. It just "is". It is part of my mind, body, soul and holistic approach. I enjoy working with the whole person as this seems to be the most authentic way to operate.'

HEALING AND INTUITION

- Intuition has been used in many traditions for healing and has played a role in medical discovery.
- Many clinicians tap into their intuition in practice; observation, communication, connecting to the client and being mindful all contribute.
- Holistic practice involves being present, attuned and having trust. These lead to transformation in therapy.
- Clinical intuition involves sensing what is happening behind the client's words and often beyond conscious awareness.
- Intuition fills the gap between theory and practice.
- One theory is that we tap into the 'universal mind' via intuition; and that the mind influences the body and healing.
- Changes occur in the brain as a result of learning and positive attitude, and visualisation is powerful.
- One model of intuitive healing involves being aware of unhelpful self-beliefs, being in touch with your body and inner energy, asking for guidance through meditation and paying attention to your dreams.

LOVE

Love is all we have, the only way that each can help the other.
EURIPIDES

Sandy's comments about Reiki lead nicely into a discussion about something that I believe is at the very essence of healing: loving-kindness. When I wrote as a child about love being like a flower, I think I had already unknowingly discovered my direction in life, that of service with loving-kindness. At times I am more aware of this than others, but when I am fully present with compassion, the healing that occurs is more profound. Robinson quotes a physician who said that 'Love is the best medicine.'[34] The love might be shared through an act of kindness, a kind word or a hug, for example.

There are some clients with whom I have been involved for fifteen to twenty years now. I know them well and there is a high level of trust between us. Sometimes knowing how they view themselves, the world or the universe helps. There is one client who has had some troubled relationships in recent years and who very much missed the consistent and loving relationship with her sister when she died. This client had been recommended to read grief books by various people but reappeared in my practice one day feeling the loss greatly.

Knowing that she believed in angels, I encouraged her to reconnect with her sister in this way. I had some cards with pictures of angels on them on my shelf. We looked at several of them together. The first card had a blue angel on it, her sister's favourite colour, and a hopeful message. My client cried and felt comforted by the words. It was as though her sister was sending her a loving message. We talked about the ways in which her sister could still be in her life. Serendipitously, another colleague was working with me that day and later said to this woman that her sister would want her to be okay because she loved her. That was just what the client needed to hear and she moved forward from that point.

Another client I have worked with for years had a very troubled childhood and became unwell as a teenager. I remember endeavouring to refer her to a specialist for review only to have one specialist say, 'No, I remember her from my hospital year and I don't want to see her.' Fortunately, I found another, more compassionate, specialist and together we were able to provide our client with consistent support. She has responded most to care with kindness and compassion, and these days is herself a caring individual, involved in her community in many different ways.

The role of intuition in love and service has been explored by a number of authors. It has been suggested that we tap into unconditional love by letting go of judgments and labelling, and see things differently by letting the heart grow. We will then become more intuitive.[35] When we give love (which is infinite), we feel 'whole', whether that is in a relationship or through volunteering. This echoes one of my favourite passages in the Bible in Corinthians 1:13, which says that love is patient and kind, never gives up and is hopeful and eternal.

You may enjoy the following meditations focusing on healing with love. The first one is by Judith Orloff.[36] I have adapted it below.

OPENING THE HEART MEDITATION

Let your eyes close and relax your body. Slowly breathe in and out; your breath provides a focal point to come back to centre.

Gently place your hand over your heart and hold it there. Now you are ready to visualise. Concentrate on a person, place or animal that you really love. For starters, it might be simpler to picture cuddling your pet or taking in a gorgeous sunset rather than focusing on a person. Whatever moves you; there is no right or wrong.

The purpose is to feel love and to notice how its energy localises in your mid-chest. Pay attention to sensations in your heart area, no matter how subtle. Warmth or tingling, expansion, compassion or joy — let it happen. Even discomfort — let it be and evolve. As you practise, allow a healing green light or a positive energy to build in your heart. This is the hub of your healing. During illness or pain, tap into it.

When you are ready, be aware of your body and your breath, and the sounds around you. Then come back to the room.

The second meditation is one that I have used for many years in my practice as many clients relate to it positively. It incorporates colour and light, and focuses on healing and love.

COLOUR MEDITATION

Make yourself comfortable and allow your eyes to close. Let the body relax from head to toe. Breathe and relax, and let the mind clear. As you go through this meditation, you can visualise the colours from a special place such as a garden or you can simply let the colours come into your mind. Or it may be that you just get a sense of the colour, rather than seeing it.

To begin with, imagine the colour blue — the blue of the

sky or the blue of the ocean; a beautiful clear blue. It is a cleansing and clearing colour. It is a good colour to begin with, to clear and cleanse the mind and body. Let the blue surround you or you can breathe it in and let it move through the mind and body to cleanse and clear away any tiredness, stress or negativity. Enjoy the colour blue.

And then meditate on the colour green. Green is the colour of trees, grass and nature. It is a healing colour. The healing of good food, of being at one with nature. Again, imagine green, visualise it if you can and surround yourself with green or breathe it in, taking it through the body, to heal … the colour green.

The next colour is pink or a pinky-red, the colour of a beautiful rose or a wonderful sunset. This is a very special colour, a colour to raise self-esteem or self-love. Surround yourself with the colour pink, an acknowledgement that each and every one of us is special, just like the rose. Take pink into your mind, into your body, into your heart. Enjoy pink and feeling good about yourself.

The next colour is a lovely golden white. It is almost like a light, the sort of light you see reflected on ocean waves on a lovely sunny day or the beams of light from a star. Imagine a white, golden light beaming towards you and let yourself receive this light. It is a special energy to refresh you and to give you energy to move forward.

And so you've experienced the cleansing of the blue, healing green, self-nurturing pinky-red, and energy from the golden white light beaming towards you. Some people like to finish with that golden white light, others like to focus on a purply-violet colour. This is a colour that is associated with the spiritual side of life. All aspects of life are important and for some people there is a spiritual context, whether that is a sense of nature or a sense of a Higher Power or God.

Imagine the colour of violets, a deep purple, and a sense of meeting spiritual needs through this colour, getting in touch with your own spirituality that's important for you. Surround yourself with this colour, a strengthening and fulfilling colour.

Spend as long as you would like enjoying the colours. When you are ready, be aware of your body, aware of the breath and the sounds around you. Then open your eyes, back in the room.

LOVE

- We will become more intuitive when we get in touch with unconditional love, and give love.
- Love is central to caring for each other.
- We can tap into love through being non-judgmental, and through service and meditation.

WISDOM

The doors of wisdom are never shut.
BENJAMIN FRANKLIN

Life is about acquiring knowledge and wisdom. Wisdom is embedded in your mind, body and spirit. In essence, you have an infinite wisdom within to tap into. It involves your intuition and allowing it to develop into its most mature form. Your inner wisdom can guide you in your everyday life and help you to align with your purpose. Intuition is also capable of generating transcendent experience. In therapy, wisdom represents the capacity to use 'the widest and deepest contexts' when working with a client, to be open and not expecting to 'know that which cannot yet be known'.[37] Clients are encouraged to recognise and use their own inner wisdom.

REFLECTIONS

I am so pleased to have been able to bring healing into this book. It is such a large part of my daily life; my purpose is wrapped up in it. I am privileged to work with people going through events in their lives and experiencing a range of emotions, to share ideas with them and to learn from them. I have learnt so much through hearing people's stories and travelling with them on their journey in life or death. Writing this chapter has reminded me of this privilege, and of the power of empowering the individual in their own healing. It has also reminded me to reconnect with having regular massages and Reiki myself!

Your 'intuition garden' journal

In your journal, answer the following questions:
1. Which ideas in this chapter resonated with you?
2. How can you apply them in your life?

FINAL WORDS

*The power of intuitive understanding will protect
you from harm until the end of your days.*
LAO TZU

When my colleagues and I teach, we often finish the session by going around the group and asking for final words from the participants about the session. Well, we have reached the end of this book about intuition and it is time for final words! The book has explored literature related to a range of disciplines and highlighted current thinking about the nature of intuition. You have been invited to view intuition from a range of perspectives and, in doing so, my hope is that you have gained some understanding of yourself and your intuition.

At the outset I said that there is more to intuition than we fully understand. I still have this view. We have been encouraged to tap into our intuition as well as our logic, to use our hearts as well as our minds, and to view intuition as a compass that can guide us in our everyday lives. We have talked about different levels of intuition and the importance of your relationship with yourself and your inner knowing. Central to developing our intuition is making space for it, through quiet times and meditation, and developing our self-awareness and creativity. A positive outlook can foster intuition, as can accessing our unconscious mind through meditation and dreams.

Keep working with the steps to enhance intuition and continue to integrate it into your everyday life. Continue, too, to be compassionate towards yourself and to show yourself the same loving-kindness that you show others.

Revisit the steps to intuition often so you remember to keep practising them:

- Make space for intuition.
- Connect with yourself and others.
- Practise meditation and mindfulness.
- Enhance your creativity.
- Access your unconscious mind.
- Tap into positivity.
- Apply intuition in your everyday and working life.

As I mentioned at the outset, writing this book required me to leave my comfort zone and to share my explorations and ideas about intuition. But at the centre of the steps to intuition is *trust*, and so I had to trust and take that leap of faith! What I have cemented in my mind is that we have a number of ways of knowing (such as intellectual, emotional and intuitive), and we can draw on the concept of 'multimodal knowing' to assist us in life. I have also discovered that there are more areas to explore for the future!

Sometimes in gardens, a plant or tree seeds and then surprises us with its appearance. As we have nurtured our intuition gardens, I think another key message has gradually grown in the garden:

When you act from your heart, intuitively, you feel interconnected with others and 'in the flow' and your action will be right for you. You will focus on what you are passionate about and find a greater sense of purpose.

I hope that you have found the key to your own intuition garden in this book, and that you will continue to nurture it in your heart and mind by using the meditations and techniques we've explored, along with your intuition journal. And enjoy it!

ACKNOWLEDGEMENTS

Thank you very much to my parents, my sisters and to my son, Alex. You have given me such joy.

Thank you also to all the individuals who shared their thoughts and experiences with me to include in this book. You are all teachers in life.

Thank you to family, friends and colleagues for being supportive of my writing.

Finally, thank you to the reader for having curiosity about intuition and exploring your intuition further.

REFERENCES

PART 1:
INTUITION THROUGH DIFFERENT LENSES

1. Bowker, K., et al., 1990, 'Intuition in the Context of Discovery', *Cognitive Psychology*, vol. 22, pp. 72–110.

2. *New World Encyclopedia*, 2008, 'Intuition', retrieved May 2011: http://www.newworldencyclopedia.org/entry/Intuition.

CHAPTER 1:
A RANGE OF DISCIPLINES

1. *New World Encyclopedia*, 2008, 'Intuition', retrieved May, 2011: http://www.newworldencyclopedia.org/entry/Intuition.

2. ibid.

3. *Standard Encyclopedia of Philosophy*, 2008, 'Kant's moral philosophy', retrieved July 2011: http://plato.stanford.edu/entries/kant-moral/.

4. *New World Encyclopedia*, loc. cit.

5. AASN Conference, Melbourne, 2007, 'Fostering the Use of Imagination in the Service of Spiritual Development', retrieved August 2012: http://www.aasn.edu.au/LinkClickaspx?fileticket=ZNdxRGeyusI%3d&tabid=88.

6. O'Connor, P., 1990, *Understanding Jung, Understanding Yourself*, Random House Australia, Melbourne, p. 24.

7. ibid., p. 80.

8. Boorstein, S., 2000, 'Transpersonal Psychotherapy', *American Journal of Psychotherapy*, vol. 54, no. 3, p. 91.

9. Firman, J. and Vargiu, J., 1977, 'Dimensions of Growth', *Synthesis*, vol. 3–4, pp. 59–119.

10. Assagioli, R., 1976, *Transpersonal Inspiration and Psychological Mountain-Climbing*, Psychosynthesis Research Foundation, New York, p. 4.

11. ibid., p. 7.

12. ibid., p. 11.

13. Myers, D.G., 2002, *Intuition: Its powers and perils*, Yale University Press, New Haven & London, p. 4.

14. ibid., p. 149.

15. ibid., p. 18.

16. Siegel, D.J., 2007, *The Mindful Brain: Reflection and attunement in the cultivation of wellbeing*, Norton & Company, New York City, p. 45.

17. Dispenza, J., 2007, *Evolve Your Brain: The science of changing your mind*, Health Communications, Inc., Florida, p. 348.

18. Myers, op. cit., p. 30.

19. Lieberman, M., 2000, 'Intuition: A social cognitive neuroscience approach', *Psychological Bulletin*, vol. 126, no. 1, pp. 109–13.

20. Myers, op. cit., p. 35.

21. Ratey, J., 2001, *A User's Guide to the Brain*, Abacus, London, p. 96.

22. Lieberman, op. cit., p. 5.

23. McNerney, S., 'The Science of Sleeping on It', retrieved July 2012: http://bigthink.com/insights-of-geniues/relaxation-creativity-the-science-of-sleeping-on-it.

24. Kim, J., 'Don't Bother Me I'm Sleeping', retrieved July 2012: http://fchornet.com/dontbothermeImsleeping-1.2872478.

25. Paul, A., 'The Science of Intuition: An eye-opening guide to your sixth sense', retrieved July 2012: http://www.oprah.com/spirit/Scientific-Facts-About-Intuition-Developing-Intuition.

26. Siegel, op. cit., p. 33.

27. ibid., p. 44.

28. Germer, C.K., 2005, 'Mindfulness: What is it? What does it matter?', *Mindfulness and psychotherapy*, C.K. Germer, R.D. Siegel and P.R. Fulton (eds), Guildford, New York, pp. 3–27

29. ibid.

30. Howell, C. and Murphy, M., 2011, *Release Your Worries: A guide to letting go of stress and anxiety*, Exisle Publishing, New South Wales, p. 57.

31. Siegel, op. cit., pp. 10, 17.

32. Farb, N., Segal, Z, Mayber, H. et al, 2007, 'Attending to the Present: Mindfulness meditation reveals distinct neural modes of self-reference', *SCAN*, vol. 2, pp. 313–22.

33. Rock, D., 2009, 'Your Brain at Work: The neuroscience of

mindfulness', *PsychologyToday*, retrieved July 2012: www.
psychologytoday.com/blog/your-brain-work/200910/the-
neuroscience-mindfulness.

34. Farb, N., Segal, Z., Mayber, H. et al., op. cit.

35. Rock, D., 2009, loc. cit.

36. Siegal, op. cit., p. 31.

37. Howell and Murphy, loc. cit.

38. Siegel, op. cit., pp. 24–5.

39. ibid., p. 30.

40. Catholic Forum, 'St Teresa of Avila: Inner Castle', retrieved August
2012: http://www.catholic-forum.com/saints/stt01001.htm.

41. Siegel, op. cit., p. 9.

42. *New World Encyclopedia*, op. cit.

43. McGreal, I.P. (ed), 1995, *Great Thinkers of the Eastern World*,
Harper Collins Publishers, New York, p. 9.

44. ibid., p. 4.

45. ibid., p. 9.

46. ibid., pp. 161–4.

47. ibid., pp. 163–5.

48. *A View on Buddhism*, 2011, 'Mind and Mental Factors',
retrieved July 2011: http://www.viewonbuddhism.org/mind.
html.

49. Wilhelm, R., 1962, *The Secret of the Golden Flower: A Chinese
book of life*, Harcourt Brace & Company, Orlando, p. 12.

50. ibid., pp. 9–12.

51. Rophet, E.C. and Spadaro, P.R., 2000, *The Art of Practical
Spirituality: How to bring more passion, creativity and balance
into everyday life*, Summit Publications, Montana, pp. 1–10.

52. *New World Encyclopedia*, op. cit.

53. Mythic Scribes. 'The Third Eye: Unleashing creative
inspiration', retrieved December 2012: http://mythicscribes.
com/inspiration/third-eye-creative-inspiration/

54. Clairvision School, 'Third Eye, the Gate that Leads Within',
retrieved December 2012: http://www.clairvision.org/about-us/
third-eye

55. *Harper's Encyclopedia of Mystical and Paranormal Experience*, 1991, 'Chakra', Castle Books, New Jersey, p. 86.

56. Mythic Scribes, op. cit.

57. Clairvision School, op. cit.

58. Wilhelm, op. cit.

59. Miovic, M., 2004, 'An Introduction to Spiritual Psychology: Overview of the literature, East and West', *Harvard Review Psychiatry*, vol. 12, pp. 105–15.

60. Internet Sacred Text Archive, 2010, 'Swedenborg', retrieved July 2011: http://www.sacred-texts.com/swd/index.htm.

61. Boorstein, op. cit., p. 410.

62. ibid.

63. *Stanford Encyclopedia of Philosophy*, 2007, 'Metaphysics', retrieved July 2011: www.plato.stanfordedu/entries/metaphysics

64. Steiner, R., 1994, *How To Know Higher Worlds*, Anthroposophic Press, Massachusetts.

CHAPTER 2:
THE ROLE OF INTUITION IN DECISION-MAKING

1. Dossey, L., 2009, *The Power of Premonitions: How knowing the future can shape our lives*, Hay House, Australia, p. xvi.

2. ibid., p. 36.

3. ibid., p. vii.

4. ibid., p. 31.

5. Welsh, I. and Lyons, C.M., 2001, 'Evidence-based Care and the Case for Intuition and Tacit Knowledge in Clinical Assessment and Decision Making in Mental Health Nursing Practice: An empirical contribution to the debate', *Journal of Psychiatric and Mental Health Nursing*, vol. 8, pp. 299–305.

6. ibid.

7. Traynor, M., Boland, M. and Buus, N., 2010, 'Autonomy, Evidence and Intuition: Nurses and decision making', *Journal of Advanced Nursing*, vol. 66, pp. 1584–91.

8. ibid.

9. Witteman, C., et al., 2009, 'Assessing Rational and Intuitive

Thinking Styles', *European Journal of Psychological Assessment*, vol. 25, pp. 39–47.

10. Welsh, I. and Lyons, C.M., op. cit.

11. Smith, A., 2009, 'Exploring the Legitimacy of Intuition as a Form of Nursing Knowledge', *Nursing Standard*, vol. 23, pp. 35–40.

12. Johansson, T. and Kroksmark, T., 2004, 'Teachers' Intuition in Action, How Teachers Experience Action', *Reflective Practice*, vol. 5, pp. 357–81.

13. ibid., p. 357.

14. ibid., p. 366.

15. Thomas, G., 2008, 'Preparing Facilitators for Experiential Education: The role of intentionality and intuition', *Journal of Adventure Education and Outdoor Learning*, vol. 8, pp. 3–20.

16. Claxton, G., 2000, 'The Anatomy of Intuition' in T. Atkinson and G. Claxton (eds), *The Intuitive Practitioner: On the value of not always knowing what one is doing*, Open University Press, Buckingham, p. 76.

17. ibid., p. 48.

18. Gladwell, M., 2005, *Blink: The power of thinking without thinking*, Penguin, Melbourne, p. 11.

19. ibid., p. 15.

20. ibid., p. 23.

21. Claxton, op. cit.

22. ibid., p. 43.

23. Dane, E. and Pratt, M.G., 2007, 'Exploring Intuition and its Role in Managerial Decision Making', *Academy of Management Review*, vol. 32, p. 36.

24. ibid., p. 47.

25. Sadler-Smith, E. and Burke, A.L., 2009, 'Fostering Intuition into Management Education: Resources and activities', *Journal of Management Education*, vol. 33, p. 243.

26. ibid., p. 249.

27. Agor, W.H., 1986, 'The Logic of Intuition: How top executives make important decisions', *Organizational Dynamics*, vol. 14, no. 3, p. 9.

28. Corey, G., 1991, *Theory and Practice of Counselling and Psychotherapy*, 4th ed., Brooks/Cole Publishing Co. California, p. 4.

29. Eisengart, S. and Faiver, C., 1996, 'Intuition in Mental Health Counseling' *Journal of Mental Health Counseling*, vol. 18, no. 1, pp. 41–52.

30. ibid.

31. Piha, H., 2004, 'Intuition: A bridge to the coenesthetic world of experience', *Journal of the American Psychoanalytic Association*, vol. 53, no. 23, p. 23.

32. Laub, L., 2006, 'Intuitive Listening', *Modern Psychoanalysis*, vol. 31, no. 1, p. 88.

33. ibid., p. 99.

34. La Quercia, T., 2005, 'Listening with the Intuitive Ear', *Modern Psychoanalysis*, vol. 30, no. 1, p. 61.

35. ibid., p. 71.

36. Rea, B.D., 2001, 'Finding Our Balance: The investigation and clinical application of intuition', *Psychotherapy*, vol. 38, no. 1, p. 105.

37. ibid.

38. ibid., p. 104.

39. Williams, S. and Irving, J., 1996. 'Intuition: A special kind of knowing?' *Counselling Psychology Quarterly*, vol. 9, no. 3, pp. 221–228.

40. Broom, A., 2009, 'Intuition, Subjectivity, and Le Bricoleur: Cancer patients' accounts of a negotiating plurality of therapeutic options', *Qualitative Health Research*, vol. 19, no. 8, p. 1050.

41. ibid., p. 1056.

42. Drydon, W. and Mytton J., 1999, *Four Approaches to Counselling*, Routledge, New York, p. 81.

43. Piha, op. cit., pp. 23–49.

CHAPTER 3:
INTUITION TYPES

1. Lewis, B. and Pucelik, F., 1990, *Magic of NLP Demystified: A pragmatic guide to communication and change*, Metamorphous Press, Oregon, p. 32.

2. Krasner, A., 1991, *The Wizard within: The Krasner Method of Clinical Hypnotherapy*, American Board of Hypnotherapy, USA, p. 56.

3. James, T. and Woodsmall, W., 1988, *Time Line Therapy and the Basis of Personality*, Meta Productions, p. 5.

4. Howell and Murphy, op. cit., p. 79.

5. ibid., p. 56.

6. Thibodeau, L., 2005, *Natural-born Intuition: How to awaken and develop your inner wisdom*, New Page Books, New Jersey, p. 37.

7. Peirce, P., 2009, *The Intuitive Way: The definitive guide to increasing your awareness*, Atria Books/Beyond Words, pp. 12–13.

8. Thibodeau, op. cit., p. 28.

9. ibid.

10. Peirce, loc. cit.

11. Thibodeau, op. cit., p. 58.

12. ibid., p. 78.

13. ibid.

14. Peirce, op. cit., p. 78.

15. Rosanoff, N., 1991, *Intuition Workout: A practical guide to discovering and developing your inner knowing*, Aslan Publishing, USA, p. 17.

CHAPTER 4:
THE SEVEN STEPS TO INTUITION

1. Thibodeau, op. cit., p. 28.

2. Gawain, S., 2000, *Developing Intuition: Practical guidance for daily life* (The Complete Book on CD), New World Library, San Rafael.

3. Howell and Murphy, op. cit., p. 29.

4. Choquette, S., 2004, *Trust Your Vibes: Secret tools for six-sensory living*, Hay House, New York, p. 10.

5. ibid., p. 93.

6. Howell and Murphy, op. cit. p. 181.

7. ibid.

8. ibid., p. 184.

9. Steiner, op. cit., p. 115.

10. ibid., pp. 122, 129.

11. Howell and Murphy, op. cit., p. 44.

12. Peirce, op. cit., p. 95.

13. ibid., p. 96.

14. Wilson, P., 2005, *Perfect Balance: Create time and space for all parts of your life*, Penguin Books, Melbourne, p. 53.

15. Crandall, L., 2011, *A Book of Simple Pleasures*, Ryland Peters & Small, London, p. 6.

16. Peirce, op. cit., pp. 17, 77.

17. Hunter M., 1988, *Daydreams for Discovery: A manual for hypnotherapists*. Sea Walk Press, West Vancouver, p. 27.

18. Dowrick, S., 2007, *Creative Journal Writing: The art and heart of reflection*, Allen & Unwin, NSW, Australia, p. 27.

19. Gawain, loc. cit.

20. ibid.

21. Orloff, J., 2010, *Emotional Freedom: Liberate yourself from negative emotions and transform your life*, Three Rivers Press, New York, p. 7.

22. Marks-Tarlow, T., 2012, *Clinical Intuition in Psychotherapy: The neurobiology of embodied response*, W.W. Norton & Company, New York, p. 42.

23. Howell and Murphy, op. cit., pp. 56–57.

24. ibid., p. 70.

25. ibid., p. 61.

26. Siegel, op. cit., p. 11.

27. Baer, R., 2003, 'Mindfulness Training as a Clinical Intervention:

A conceptual and empirical review', *Clinical Psychology: Science and practice*, vol. 10, no. 2, pp. 125–42.

28. Harris, R., 2010, 'Mindfulness', retrieved July 2012: www.actmindfully.com.au/mindfulness.

29. Harris, R., 2009, 'Mindfulness Without Meditation', *Journal of Clinical Psychology*, October 2009, pp. 21–4.

30. Howell and Murphy, op. cit.

31. Labryrinth Society of Edmonton, 2011, 'Basic Approaches to Walking the Labyrinth', retrieved September 2011: www.ualberta.ca/-cbidwell/SITES/labways.htm.

32. Choquette, S., 2008, *The Answer is Simple ... Love Yourself, Live Your Spirit*, Hay House, New York, p. 112.

33. Runco, M. and Jaegar, G., 2012, 'The Standard Definition of Creativity', *Creativity Research Journal*, vol. 21, p. 92.

34. Mumford, M.D., 2003, 'Where Have We Been, Where Are We Going? Taking stock in creativity research', *Creativity Research Journal*, vol. 15, p. 110.

35. Thibodeau, op. cit., p. 35.

36. Policastro, E., 1995, 'Creative Intuition: An integrative review', *Creativity Research Journal*, vol. 8, no. 2, p. 100.

37. Russell, D., 1981, 'Psychosynthesis in Western Psychology', retrieved October 2010: http://two.not2.org/psychosynthesis/articles/pd1-1.htm.

38. The Will Parfitt Website, 'What is Psychosynthesis?', retrieved October 2010: http://www.willparfitt.com/whatispslong.html.

39. Helie, S. and Sun, R., 'Incubation, Insight and Creative Problem-solving: A unified theory and a connectionist model', retrieved April 2012, http://www.psych.ucsb.edu/-ashby/HelieSunEII.pdf.

40. Policastro, loc. cit.

41. Eubanks, D.L., Murphy, S.T. and Mumford, M.D., 2010, 'Intuition as an Influence on Creative Problem-solving: The effects of intuition, positive affect, and training', *Creativity Research Journal*, vol. 22, no. 2, pp. 170–84.

42. Marks-Tarlow, op. cit., p. 176.

43. Howell and Murphy, op. cit., p. 168.

44. The Future Buzz, 2008, 'How to be More Creative', retrieved

30 July 2011: http://thefuturebuzz.com/200812/22/how-to-be-more-creative/.

45. ibid.

46. Kennedy, S.A.R., 2005, *Sark's New Creative Companion: Ways to free your creative spirit*, Celestial Arts, California, p. 24.

47. Choquette, 2008, loc. cit.

48. ibid., p. 18.

49. Dowrick, op. cit., p. 143.

50. Dr Hein's Virtual Viewing, 2010, 'How to Access Your Creativity', retrieved 30 July 2011: http://virtualviewing.org/learningcreativity.html.

51. Malchiodi, C., 1998, *The Art Therapy Sourcebook*, Lowell House, Los Angeles, p. 119.

52. Brown, M.H., 2001, 'A Psychosynthesis Twelve-Step Program for Transforming Consciousness: Creative explorations of inner space', *Journal of Counseling and Values*, vol. 45, no. 2, pp. 103–17.

53. ibid.

54. Tenzin-Dolma, L., 2008, *Healing Mandalas: 30 inspiring meditations to soothe your mind, body & soul*, Duncan Baird, London, p. 75.

55. ibid., p. 14.

56. *Harper's Encyclopedia of Mystical and Paranormal Experience*, loc. cit.

57. ibid.

58. Orloff, J., 2000, *Dr Judith Orloff's Guide to Intuitive Healing: 5 steps to physical, emotional and sexual wellness*, Three Rivers Press, USA, p. 30.

59. Virtue, D., 2004, *Chakra Clearing: Awakening your spiritual power to know and heal*, Hay House, New York, p. 17.

60. Orloff, 2000, op. cit.

61. Dowrick, op. cit., p. 48.

62. Harris, R., 2009, *ACT Made Simple: A quick-start guide to ACT basics and beyond*, New Harbinger publications, Inc., p. 10.

63. Dimeff, L. and Koerner K. (eds), 2007, *Dialectical Behaviour*

Therapy in Clinical Practice Applications Across Disorders and Settings, The Guilford Press, New York, p. 158.

64. Harris, loc. cit.

65. McKay, M., Wood, C.J. and Brantley, J., 2007, *The Dialectical Behavior Therapy Skills Workbook*, New Harbinger Publications, California.

66. Peirce, op. cit., pp. 21–5.

67. Dowrick, op. cit., p. 147.

68. Fontana, D., 1994, *The Secret Language of Symbols: A visual key to symbols and their meanings*, Chronicle Books, p. 21.

69. ibid.

70. Peirce, op. cit., p. 132.

71. Ness, C., 2006, *Secrets of Dreams*, The Ivy Press, United Kingdom, p. 8.

72. O'Connor, op. cit., p. 176.

73. Ness, op. cit., p. 52.

74. ibid., p. 27.

75. ibid., p. 175.

76. Dossey, op. cit., p. 12.

77. Orloff, 2000, op. cit., p. 95.

78. ibid.

79. Fredrickson, B., 2009, *Positivity: Groundbreaking reseach to release your inner optimist and thrive,* Oneworld, Oxford, p. 12.

80. ibid., p. 197.

81. Bloom, W., 2011,*The Power of Modern Spirituality: How to live a life of compassion and personal fulfillment*, Piatkus, Great Britain.

82. Howell and Murphy, op. cit., p. 220.

83. Orloff, J. and Chopra, D., 2001, *The Power of Intuition* (CD), Hay House Audio.

84. King, E., 'Kind: The word that can change your life', *Sunday Mail*, 11 September 2011, p. 6.

85. Bloom, op. cit., p. 85.

86. Neff, K., 2003, 'Self-compassion: An alternative

conceptualisation of a healthy attitude toward oneself', *Self and Identity*, vol. 2, p. 86.

87. Howell and Murphy, op. cit., p. 222.

88. Frederickson, op. cit., p. 209.

89. Pelletier, A.M., 1990, 'Ego-strengthening: Enhancing esteem, self-efficacy, and confidence — The Prominent Tree metaphor', *Handbook of Hypnotic Suggestions and Metaphors*, D.C. Hammond (ed.), Norton & Co, New York, p. 139.

90. Lyubomirsky, S., 2007, *The How of Happiness: A scientific approach to getting the life you want*, Penguin Press HC, London, p. 88.

91. Hadgraft, B., 2011, 'Paralysed Marie-Therese finished her love list to life days before dying', *Sunday Mail*, 4 September 2011, p. 10.

92. Lyubomirsky, op. cit., p. 92.

93. ibid., p. 95.

94. Orloff, 2000, op. cit., p. xv.

95. Orloff, J., 1997, *Awakening Second Sight* (CD), Sounds True.

96. *Collins Australian Pocket Dictionary*, 2005, 'Passion', HarperCollins Publishers, Great Britain.

97. Adrienne, C., 1998, *The Purpose of Your Life: Finding your place in the world using synchronicity, intuition and uncommon sense*, Thornsons, London, p. 271.

98. Hillman, C., 1992, *Recovery of Your Self-Esteem: A guide for women*, Fireside, New York, pp. 75–8.

99. James, T. and James, A., 2011, *Time-Line Therapy Practitioner Training*, Adelaide.

100. Orloff, 1997, loc. cit.

101. Adrienne, loc. cit.

102. Orloff, 2000, op. cit., p. 10.

103. Marks-Tarlow, loc. cit.

104. Peirce, op. cit., pp. 97–8.

105. Orloff, 1997, loc. cit.

106. Orloff, 2000, op. cit., p. 11.

107. Rosanoff, op. cit., p. 39.

108. ibid., p. 41.

109. Choquette, op. cit., p. 97.

110. Rosanoff, op. cit., p. 58.

111. http://www.reggiokids.com/about/hundred_languages.php.

112. Howell and Murphy, op. cit., p. 55.

113. Peirce, op. cit., p. 25.

114. Rosen, R., 2011, *Spirited: Unlock your psychic self and change your life*, Harper Perennial, New York, p. 107.

CHAPTER 5:
SYNCHRONICITY, PREMONITIONS AND THE THIRD EYE

1. Chopra, D., 2003, *Synchrodestiny: Harnessing the infinite power of coincidence to create miracles*, Random House Group Limited, London, p. 23.

2. ibid., p. 138.

3. ibid., p. 141.

4. ibid., p. 22.

5. Dossey, op. cit., p. 2.

6. ibid., p. 67.

7. ibid., p. 17.

8. ibid, p. 63.

9. ibid., p. 92.

10. ibid., p. 67.

11. ibid., p. 106.

12. ibid., pp. 130–3.

13. Gallagher, S., 'Spirituality and Meditation: The most powerful meditation technique to open the third eye chakra', retrieved 29 December 2012: http://www.mymeditationgarden.com/meditation-techniques/chakra-meditation.

14. Mudashram Insitute of Spiritual Studies, 'How to Open Your Third Eye', retrieved 29 December 2012: http://mudrasharam.com/thirdeye.html.

15. Parker, J., 'A Third Eye Meditation to Open Your Psychic Ability', retrieved 29 December 2012: http://www.jonathanparker.org/jonathans-blog/meditation/third-eye-meditation.

CHAPTER 6:
HEALING

1. Wallace, B.A., 2005, *Genuine Happiness: Meditation as the path to fulfillment*, John Wiley and Sons, New York, p. 95.

2. Berlingieri, J., 2006, 'A Gathering of Small Knowings: An artistic inquiry into the experience of using intuition in creative arts therapy', Exhibition and Exegesis, Master of Arts, retrieved September 2012: http://www.miecat.org.au/pdf/textorium/mas_jb_2006.pdf p.5.

3. *The Advertiser*, 'Birth of a New TV Hit: Thumbs up for this baby', 2 September 2012, p. 25.

4. Rogers as quoted in the art therapy thesis p. 37, from Eisengart and Faiver, 1996, 'Intuition in Mental Health Counselling', *Journal of Mental Health*, vol. 18, no. 1, p. 44.

5. Siegel, D.J., 2010, *The Mindful Therapist: A clinician's guide to mindsight and neural integration*, Norton & Company, New York City, p. xxv.

6. ibid., p. 44.

7. ibid., p. xx.

8. ibid., p. xxiii.

9. ibid., p. xxv.

10. ibid., p. 236.

11. Marks-Tarlow, op. cit., p. xiii.

12. ibid., p. 3.

13. ibid., p. 42.

14. ibid., p. 11.

15. ibid., p. 18.

16. ibid., p. 56.

17. Orloff and Chopra, loc. cit.

18. Hamilton, D., 2010, *How Your Mind Can Heal Your Body*, Hay House Inc., New York. p. 17.

19. ibid., p. 5.

20. ibid., p. 25.

21. ibid., p. 7.

22. ibid., p. 38.

23. ibid., p. 42.

24. ibid., p. 45.

25. ibid., p. 57.

26. ibid., p. 65.

27. ibid., p. 77.

28. Robinson, op. cit., p. 91.

29. Orloff, 2000, op. cit., p. 8.

30. ibid., p. 134.

31. ibid., p. 133.

32. ibid., p. 37.

33. ibid., p. 41.

34. Robinson, op. cit., p. 167.

35. Orloff and Chopra, loc. cit.

36. Orloff, 2000, op. cit., p. 85.

37. Marks-Tarlow, op. cit., p. 219.

INDEX

A

A Book of Simple Pleasures (book) 79
Acceptance and Commitment Therapy (ACT) 69
Accessing your intuition meditation 135
'adaptive unconscious' 34
affirmations 119, 174
Agor, Weston 36
amygdala 16
anterior cingulate cortex 20
art therapy 164–5
Assagioli, Roberto 13–14, 45
auditory sense 45–7, 51–2
Aurobindo, Sri 26
author's experience
    approach to therapy 166–7
    beliefs 143–4
    death of mother 78–9
    dreams 111–13, 124, 157
    early writing 114–15
    first book rejection 75–6
    intuition 30, 80–1
    signs 109–10
awareness, intuitive 170
Awareness of intuition meditation 84

B

balance, body, mind and spirit 77–9
basal ganglia 16
'being there' frame of mind
    of teachers 33–4
    see also mindfulness
beliefs
    author's experience 143–4
    effect on purpose 127
    during illness 174–5
    unhelpful, unconscious 143

body, mind and spirit
    balance 77–9
    connection with 74–6, 171–3
brain
    circuits 19–20
    cortex 17, *18*, 19
    function during sleep 16–18
    left and right hemispheres 15–16, 27
    structure 15–17, *18*
brain wave patterns 46
breathing meditation 89–90
'bricolage' 40
Broom, Alex 39
Buddhism 23–4
business decision-making 35–7

C

cancer, and visualisation 173–4
CBT (Cognitive Behaviour Therapy) 127, 143
chakra system 101, 159–61
children, intuitive 141–2
Chopra, Deepak 116, 151, 171
Choquette, Sonia 66
Claxton, Guy 34–5
Cognitive Behaviour Therapy (CBT) 127, 143
coincidences 151–5
collective unconscious 13, 111–14
Colour meditation 180–2
comparison, with others 117
compassion 114–22
Confucius 23
connection
    with body, mind and spirit 74–6, 171–3
    with self and others 68–9, 86

conscious self 105
cortex, brain 17, *18*, 19
The cottage and garden meditation 55–6
counselling, and intuition 37–9
Crandall, Leigh 79
creative activities 98
creativity
  concept explained 93–4
  developing 94–8
  enhancing 93, 103
  meditation 98–9

D
Dane, Eric 35–6
DBT (Dialectical Behaviour Therapy) 105
de-cluttering
  life's old stories 66–8
  mind and life 63–5
  summary *18*
decision-making
  assistance with 135
  in business 35–7
  meditations for 136–8
  in nursing 31–3
  rapid 34
  in teaching 34–5
Dialectical Behaviour Therapy (DBT) 105
direct experience circuit (brain) 20
Donaldson, Mary 152
Dossey, Larry 30, 155
Dowrick, Rev. Dr Stephanie 83
dreams
  author's experience 111–13, 124, 157
  children's 141–2
  human need for 110–13
  interpreting 112
  paying attention to 123–4, 175
  premonitory 111, 157

risk of ignoring 112
'dual processing' 15

E
Eastern philosophies 22–8
Eat Pray Love (book) 78
Einstein, Albert 94
Eisengart, Sheri 37
Emotional Freedom (book) 85
empathy 39, 85–6
Enjoying nature meditation 88–9
expectations, letting go of 144

F
Faiver, Christopher 37
falls, history behind 29–30
fear
  effect of 141
  exercises for letting go 145–6
feelings vs thoughts 143
First sensory meditation 49
Frankl, Victor 172

G
garden, regeneration analogy 8
Gautarna, Siddhartha 23
Gawain, Shakti 83
Gladwell, Malcolm 34
goalsetting 73
gratitude, practising 120–2
gratitude journal 122
guided imagery *see* visualisation
gut-feelings 131–2

H
Hamilton, David 171–3
happiness, searching for 78
Hay, Louise 119
healing
  author's intuitive approach 166–7
  and intuition 163–77

health care, intuition in 31–2
'hedonic adaptation' 122
Helfgott, David 172–3
Higher Self 27, 104–6, 161
hippocampus 19
hypnosis 46
hypnotherapy 173–4
  vs hypnosis 46
  visualisation 173–4

I
ideomotor finger signals 106
imagination 14
'in the flow' term 84
Indeterminacy/Technicality ratio 31
'inner critic' 127
'inner eye' 14, 26
inner guidance, asking for 134
'The inner smile' meditation 116–17
inner voice 132–3
Instilling positives and letting go of
  negatives meditation 145–6
insula (brain) 20
intelligence, emotional 14
intuition
  applying in life 139
  author's experience 80–1
  and children 141–2
  clinical 169, 172
  and counselling 37–9
  definition 8–9
  Eastern approaches 22–5
  emotional 54–7
  everyday application 130–47
  four characteristics 35–6
  and healing 163–77, 174–7
  medical school training 155–6
  and nursing 40
  and philosophy 11–12
  and psychology 13–14, 15–17
  and psychotherapy 37–9

questions about 3
and religion 21–2
and the senses 49–54
social 16
and spirituality 25–6
and teaching 33–5, 40
three primary modes 54
and trust 140–1
types of 45–6, 57
  see also seven step model of
    intuition
intuitive awareness 170

J
journalling
  getting started 6
  gratitude journal 122
  suggested method 80
  tapping into intuition 138–9
Jung, Carl
  collective unconscious 13, 104,
    111–14
  dream interpretations 111–12
  four modalities of experience 14

K
Kabat-Zinn, Jon 19, 90
Kant, Immanuel 12
Kierkegaard, Seren 12
kinaesthetic sense 45–7, 54–7
kindness *see* loving-kindness
knowing, ways of 19

L
La Quercia, Theodora 38
labyrinths 92
Lamb, Lynne 37–8
leather work therapy 95
left brain hemisphere 15, 27
letter writing 105–6
light, meditation on 133–4

listening
  intuitively 37–8
  to thoughts and inner voice 132–3
  to your body 131–2
'locked in' syndrome, living with 121
love
  healing power of 178
  and intuition 182
loving-kindness, improves our
  wellbeing 116
Loving-kindness meditation 115,
  118–19
loving-kindness poem 118

M
Madonna (entertainer) 109
management, decision-making 35–7
mandalas 99–102
Marks-Tarlow (psychologist) 169
Mary, Crown Princess of Denmark 170
Maslow, Abraham 81, 94
material belongings 64
medical school training 155–6
meditation
  for decision-making 136–8
  developing creativity 98–9
  explained 48
  guidance through 133, 175
  practice of 87–90, 92
meditation examples
  Accessing your intuition meditation
    135
  Awareness of intuition meditation
    84
  Breathing meditation 89–90
  Colour meditation 180–2
  The cottage and garden meditation
    55–6
  Creativity meditation 98–9
  Enjoying nature meditation 88–9
  First sensory meditation 49

'The inner smile' meditation 116–17
Instilling positives and letting go of
  negatives meditation 145–6
Loving-kindness meditation 115,
  118–19
Meditation on light 133–4
Meditation on the third eye 160–1
Mindfulness meditation 91
Opening the heart meditation
  179–80
Path meditation 137–8
Personal symbol meditation 109
Remembering coincidences
  meditation 154
Reviewing daily coincidences
  meditation 153
Second sensory meditation 55–6
Sensing the third eye meditation
  159
Single box for de-cluttering 65
on spirit 77
Three bucket meditation 82–3
Tree meditation 119–20
'Yes' or 'no' meditation 136
mental intuition 54–7
mindfulness 19–21, 87, 90–2, 167–9,
  171
Mindfulness meditation 91
'mindsight' 168
multimodal therapy 81
music, life's passion 47

N
narrative circuit (brain) 19–20
negative images, in meditation 145–6
negative/positive self-belief 127–8
negative stories 66–7
Neuro-Linguistic Programming (NLP)
  45–6
neurobiology 17, 169
neuroplasticity 20, 172

nursing
  decision-making styles 31–3
  and intuition 40

O

Opening the heart meditation 179–80
Orloff, Judith
  childhood dreams and premonitions
    123
  intuitive healing 155–6, 174–5
owls, symbol of wisdom 110

P

pain management 174
PART acronym 168
Path meditation 137–8
Peirce, Penney 62, 64, 105
pendulums 106
person-centred therapy 166–7
Personal symbol meditation 109
philosophy
  Eastern approaches 22–8
  and intuition 11–12
Piha, Heikki 37, 39
positivity
  improved immune system 171
  from the negative 127–8
  tapping into 114–30
Pratt, Michael 35–6
prayer
  forms of 22
  value of 27
prefrontal cortex 17, 18, 19
premonitions 155–8
'presentiment' 156
psychology
  early 14
  and intuition 13–14, 15–17
  modern 15–17, 18
psychosynthesis 13, 81
psychotherapeutic approaches 106

psychotherapy, and intuition 37–9
purpose, finding 123–30

R

Radin, Dean 156
random acts of kindness 117
Rea, Bayard Doge 38
Reiki 176
relationships, importance of 85
relaxation techniques 89
religion, and intuition 21–2
REM sleep 17
Remembering coincidences
  meditation 154
Reviewing daily coincidences
  meditation 153
right brain hemisphere 16, 27
Robinson, Sir Ken 174
role models 126
Rosanoff, Nancy 136
Rosen, Rebecca 145

S

'sacred circles' 99–102
Schleiermacher, Friedrich 24
Second sensory meditation 55–6
'second sight' 155–8
The Secret Garden (book) 7–8
The Secret of the Golden Flower
  (Chinese text) 23
self, terms for 117
self-actualisation 81
self-assessment 127
self-awareness 79–85
self-belief 127–8
self-care 65–6
self-compassion 117
self-criticism 147
senses, and intuition 49–54
Sensing the third eye meditation 159
seven step model of intuition

applying intuition 130–47
connection 68–86
creativity 93–103
diagram *62*
making space 63–8
meditation and mindfulness 87–91
positivity 127–45
unconscious mind access 104–13
Siegel, Dan 167–9
signs 109–10
sleep
brain function 16–17
dreams 157–8
REM stage 17
Smith, Anita 32
spirit
connection with 74–6
Latin origins of word 25
meditation on 77
spirituality, and intuition 25–6
Steiner, Rudolf 12, 68
stories, negative 66–7
Swedenborg, Emmanuel 26
symbols
in dreams 111–13
examples 107–8, 111
use of 108
synchronicity 151–5

T
Taoism 23
teaching with intuition 40, 33–5
third eye 25–6, 159–61, 161
Thomas, G 34
thoughts
vs feelings 143
paying attention to 132–3, 139
Thredbo landslide 157
The three bucket meditation 82–3
transpersonal psychology 13–14, 27
Traynor, Michael 32

Tree meditation 119–20
trust, developing 139–44, 147

U
unconscious mind 104–6, 113, 169,
173–4

V
values, personal 69–72
visual sense 45–7, 50–1
visualisation
healing cancer 173–4
healing using 173
improving performance 172–3
use in hypnotherapy 173

W
Welsh, Ian 32
Williams, Sheryl 38–9
wisdom 182–3
writing
author's young experience 114–15
of fears and negative thoughts 144
letters 105–6
tapping into intuition 138–9
see also journalling

Y
'Yes or no' meditation 136